YOUR DOODLE'S DAILY SCHEDULE BLUEPRINT

FROM HYPER TO HAPPY:
PROVEN ROUTINES FOR A CALMER, HAPPIER DOODLE

By
CORINNE GEARHART,
THE DOODLE PRO®

Published by

The Doodle Pro® Academy Publishing

ISBN: 979-8-9926055-0-1 **First Edition:** May 2025 **Printed in the United States of America**

Art Credits

Cover illustration by **Putnum Road Art**. Cover design by **Muhammad Arslan Ahmad**. Author bio photos by **Upstreet Photography Headshots**. Childhood picture of the author courtesy of the author. Illustrations and infographics created using **Canva Pro** under a commercial license.

Disclaimer

The information provided in this book is based on the author's professional experience and research. It is not intended to replace professional veterinary, training, or medical advice. Readers are encouraged to consult a qualified veterinarian, certified dog trainer, or other canine professional for specific concerns regarding their dogs.

Media Attribution

The logos featured on the cover represent media outlets where the author, Corinne Gearhart, has been featured. These outlets have not reviewed or endorsed this book.

For additional resources, training support, and expert insights, visit: **thedoodlepro.com**

To Ethan and Gavin,

to Nestlé,

in loving memory of Hershey,

and to every family who entrusted me to

love their pups as my own.

Are you a Doodle breeder?

I created a complimentary **Breeder Bonus Kit** just for ethical Doodle programs who want to give their puppy families confident, science-based guidance from Day 1.

Scan below or visit TheDoodlePro.com/BreederBonus to claim your kit.

Scan me

Contents

Acknowledgements

To my sons, Ethan and Gavin—your love, laughter, and belief in me have been my greatest motivation. Thank you for being my biggest supporters, for understanding the long hours, and for reminding me of what truly matters.

To my **ShedFreeStay™ family**—you have been by my side through countless Doodle adventures, and your trust in me has meant everything. This book is, in many ways, a reflection of the work and experiences we've shared.

To my community—the **Building Blocks, Denver Sunflowers, and CCV Women**—your friendship, humor, and unwavering support have given me strength through every step of this journey. You've taught me to see life's peaks from its valleys, and I am deeply grateful for the communities we've built together.

To my **family and loved ones**—thank you for tolerating my endless talk about dogs, our home filled with Doodles during holidays and family gatherings, and understanding when I couldn't travel because of my commitment to caring for these beloved pups. Your support of this path means everything to me.

To the **Academy for Dog Trainers**—you have taught me so much, and I still have so much to learn from you. Your dedication to evidence-based training has influenced my work in ways I will always be grateful for.

To the **authors and trainers** whose work has shaped my understanding—**Jean Donaldson, Malena DeMartini-Price, Dr. Zazie Todd, Laura Monaco Torelli, Suzanne Clothier, and Dr. Karen Overall**—your research, writing, and expertise have profoundly impacted my approach. From the first time I picked up *Mine!* to learning about relaxation techniques and humane behavior modification, your knowledge has guided me at every stage of my career.

To all my **podcast guests**—thank you for sharing your expertise with our community. Your willingness to share your knowledge and experiences has enriched our understanding of positive dog training.

To the **groomers, trainers, breeders, and Doodle parents** in the **Doodle Insider Team** who shared their experiences and provided feedback—your stories helped refine this book and ensure that it meets the real-world needs of Doodle families.

To my **childhood self**—the one who devoured every book about dogs she could find—I still can't believe I now have one among them.

Introduction

Why This Book Will Change the Way You Raise Your Doodle

A Resource You'll Return to Again and Again

"I love my Doodle, but..."

If you've ever whispered this after a long day, you're not alone. Maybe your Doodle is a mischievous sock thief, a zoomie tornado at 9 p.m., or a bark-on-command coworker during work meetings.

Perhaps you've invested in training, watched all the videos, and followed the advice—but your Doodle still seems one step ahead of you.

Or maybe you're exhausted from puppyhood, feeling overwhelmed by potty training and crate whining. Or your adolescent Doodle has suddenly forgotten every rule they once knew.

If this sounds familiar, take a deep breath. You're not failing—your Doodle simply needs a different approach. One designed specifically for their intelligence, energy, and emotional depth.

The Doodle Parent Reality Check

That was exactly what Luke's mom, Alexis, experienced. She told me:

"Before I found The Doodle Pro®'s training methods, things were a bit chaotic with Luke. I've always loved him, but back then... I didn't like him very much! He was getting into things he shouldn't (a pro counter-surfer!) and just testing my limits like a typical toddler pup. After following Corinne's approach, I finally felt like I had a handle on things—and could enjoy my Doodle again."
—Alexis D., The Doodle Pro® Academy Graduate

Doodle parents like Alexis aren't alone. Doodles aren't like other dogs. They're different—wonderfully so.

And that's why they need a completely different approach to training, structure, and daily life.

Unlike other breeds, Doodles are a blend of intelligence, energy, and emotional sensitivity—a combination that makes them amazing companions, but also overwhelming without the right structure.

This book isn't just about surviving puppyhood or fixing one behavior issue—it's a **long-term resource** that you can return to as your Doodle matures, life or schedules change, or when (let's be honest) you add another Doodle—because they're like Lay's chips: you can't have just one. You'll find yourself returning to different chapters as your Doodle grows from puppy to adolescent to adult, adapting the schedules to match their changing needs and energy levels throughout their lifespan.

This book isn't about training harder, exercising more, or "fixing" behaviors. It's about working with your Doodle's nature instead of against it—so you can both thrive together.

Before we dive in, I want to clarify what makes this book different. **Your Doodle's Daily Schedule Blueprint™** focuses on *when, not how.* You'll learn the daily schedules, routines, and rhythms that create balance and predictability for your Doodle. While I'll occasionally mention basic techniques, this isn't a comprehensive training manual—it's your scheduling blueprint, your roadmap for *when* to structure activities throughout the day to prevent common Doodle challenges before they start. The right schedule creates the foundation that makes all other training more effective.

A Bonus Gift Just for You

To help you implement everything in this book, I've created **The Doodle Daily Toolkit**™—a free, reader-exclusive companion resource. It includes printable daily schedules, training guides, and expert checklists to help set you and your Doodle up for success.

Turn the page to grab your free toolkit and start building the routine your Doodle needs.

A Note for Readers

If this book looks like the resource you've been searching for—or you think other Doodle families would find it helpful—please consider leaving a review on Amazon. Just one line helps other Doodle parents discover this resource.

thedoodlepro.com/amazonreview

Share your feedback on Amazon

Before You Start

Your Exclusive Doodle Daily Toolkit™

DAILY DOODLE TOOLKIT™
DIGITAL DOWNLOAD

Before You Start: Unlock Your Exclusive Doodle Daily Toolkit™

To help you put this Blueprint into action, I've created the **Doodle Daily Toolkit™**—a complimentary, reader-only bonus with done-for-you tools to make your Doodle's routine easier to follow (and easier to stick with).

Whether you're navigating puppy chaos, adolescent testing, or family schedule shifts, these print-and-post templates keep everyone on the same page—literally.

What's Inside:

- **Printable Routine Posters:** The Doodle Morning Flow™, Midday Reset™, & Wind-Down Plans™—ready to post on your fridge or clipboard for quick reference.
- **Potty & Housetraining tools:** Easy-to-follow Potty Timing Charts and a customizable Housetraining Log to track success and prevent setbacks.
- **Daily Schedule Templates:** Plug-and-play guides for Work-from-Home life,

Boarding Recovery, and the Adolescent Doodle Daily Rhythm.

• **Health & Grooming Trackers:** Vet Care Logs and Grooming Schedules to stay organized and keep your Doodle thriving.

• **Socialization Success Kit:** Includes The Doodle Puppy Socialization Blueprint™ and a checklist-style tracker for confidence-building adventures.

• **The Flexible Rhythm Blueprint™:** Build calm routines for Doodle families with hybrid work, travel sports, shift schedules, or just unpredictable days.

• **Reader-Only Discounts:** Curated tools and supplies I personally use and recommend

• **... plus a few extra surprises to make your Doodle's days calmer and your life easier.**

Designed to print and post on your fridge, wall, or clipboard—so everyone's on the same page.

Visit thedoodlepro.com/bonustoolkit or scan the QR code below to download instantly. All printable resources referenced throughout this book can be found in this exclusive reader-only package.

Scan this QR code with your smartphone camera to download.

What You'll Learn in This Book

You don't need a rigid training program or hours of daily exercise.
You need a schedule that works with your Doodle's natural instincts.

Important Reminder: This schedule is your home base, not your leash. You can absolutely go off-script for hikes, beach days, or play-all-day daycare, and then return to this rhythm to bring the calm back home. This Blueprint isn't about control; it's about consistency when it counts.

This book will show you how to create a predictable, adaptable daily flow that prevents behavior problems before they start:

- **The Doodle Morning Flow™, Midday Reset™, and Wind-Down Plan™**
  Step-by-step daily rhythms that promote calm, not chaos

- **The Doodle Puppy & Adolescent Schedules**
  Life-stage structure that grows with your Doodle

- **Potty Training & Crate Comfort Schedules**
  How to build reliable habits and teach your Doodle to settle

- **The Doodle Socialization Blueprint™**
  How to raise a confident pup—without overstimulation

- **Real-Life Routines**
  Structure for work-from-home life, travel, boarding, and transitions

This isn't just a collection of tips—it's a **Doodle-specific framework** designed to set you up for success.

One Last Note Before We Begin...

Throughout this book, you'll meet real Doodles and their families. To respect their privacy, I've changed their names—because even Doodles deserve a little anonymity .But rest assured, every story, challenge, and training success you'll read is **100% real**.

You'll also see tips and real-world insights from Doodle parents, breeders, and pet professionals I've learned from along the way. Their inclusion is meant to reflect shared experiences— not necessarily a full endorsement of every method or philosophy. As always, take what resonates with you and your Doodle, and feel free to leave the rest.

By the End of This Book, You'll Have:

- **Practical Tools**: A customizable daily schedule framework that adapts to your lifestyle while meeting your Doodle's unique needs.

- **Daily Balance**: Clear guidance on the right mix of mental enrichment, physical exercise, and structured downtime your Doodle craves.

- **Behavior Insights**: A deeper understanding of why Doodles respond differently to traditional training methods and how to work with their natural tendencies.

Next Up: Meet Your Guide

You've already taken the first step—**recognizing that Doodles need a different approach**.

Now, let's meet your guide—and talk about why I'm so passionate about helping Doodle parents like you.

Meet Your Guide

From Dog-Obsessed Kid to The Doodle Pro®

I 'm sharing the real story behind how I became The Doodle Pro®—and why I know exactly what you're going through.

I've spent more than 50,000 *hours* working one-on-one with Doodles—training, boarding, and coaching their devoted parents. I've worked with puppies, adolescents, adults, and rescues, and I've seen firsthand what works—and what doesn't.

But my journey began long before I became *The Doodle Pro®*— before I ever had a dog of my own.

Me at age six, with one of my many beloved stuffed dogs.

From Childhood Obsession to a Lifelong Calling

As a child, I wrote to Santa every single year, begging for a puppy. I promised I'd keep it in my room so my allergic mother wouldn't have an asthma attack. Every toy, every book—everything I loved—centered around dogs.

I know what it's like to want a dog more than anything.

And I know what it's like to finally bring one home—only to realize that love alone doesn't make life with a high-energy, intelligent dog any easier.

The Dogs Who Shaped My Journey

My first dog, Hershey, a *Standard Poodle*, unlocked my destiny to have dogs in my life. She showed me firsthand what makes the Poodle side of Doodles so unique—their brilliance, their sensitivity, and their deep need for connection.

Today, my *Cavapoo, Nestlé* (yes, also named after chocolate like Hershey), continues to teach me just how special these dogs are. Every day, he reminds me why Doodles aren't just "another breed" of dog.

These personal experiences with both a Poodle and a Poodle mix, combined with thousands of hours working specifically with Doodle crosses of all varieties, gave me a deep understanding of what makes these dogs truly unique—and what they need to thrive.

They don't just want to be near you—they need consistency and reassurance to feel safe and secure.

Maybe you also chose a Doodle because of allergies, cleanliness, or simply because you wanted a **real-life teddy bear** in your life.

No matter how you got here, **you and your Doodle were meant to find each other—just like I was meant to find mine.**

Why Love Alone Isn't Enough

After personally working with *hundreds of Doodles—and caring for them across thousands of overnight stays*—I've learned one undeniable truth:

- Love alone isn't enough.

- These brilliant, social, high-energy dogs need *guidance and predictable rhythms* to thrive.

That's why I developed **The Doodle Daily Blueprint™**—a flexible, science-backed framework designed specifically for Doodles.

Through **ShedFreeStay™**, my specialized, Doodle-exclusive boarding program, I had a rare opportunity—an almost decade-long, real-world study on what truly helps Doodles *settle, learn, and adjust to change.*

What I Learned From Thousands of Doodles

I didn't just teach schedules—I *tested them, tracked patterns,* and *refined them daily* with *hundreds of Doodles* of all ages, sizes, and mixes. Over *thousands of overnights* and through my **Doodle Pro Academy® courses and podcast**, I observed what truly worked.

At first, I focused on solving everyday behavior struggles—restlessness, separation anxiety, overstimulation, demand barking. But over time, I realized something even more valuable:

Predictable rhythms didn't just create calmer dogs day to day—they gave Doodles a built-in buffer to adjust when life changed.

- **A sudden schedule shift?** Dogs with consistent routines adapted faster.

- **A family vacation?** Dogs with predictable rest and activity rhythms settled into new places more easily.

- **A change in their home environment?** Dogs who had daily structure found their footing again with less stress.

That's the beauty of **The Doodle Daily Blueprint™**—it's not about rigid rules. It's about creating a rhythm that helps your Doodle feel secure, *even when things change.*

Why This Book Is Different

This book brings together the best of both worlds:

- **Real-world boarding experience** (*thousands of Doodles, real-life schedules*).

- **Real-life Doodle parent coaching** (*what actually works in a home setting*).

So you can *skip the trial and error* and go straight to *what works*.

- **Brand-new puppy?** You'll set them up with predictable structure from day one.

- **Adolescent Doodle who never "grew out of it"?** You'll finally have a clear daily schedule that makes life easier.

- **Adult or rescue Doodle?** You'll know how to adapt their routine for long-term success.

I've worked with thousands of Doodles. I wrote this because I saw too many great dogs being misunderstood—and too many amazing families thinking they were failing. You're not. And this book is your step-by-step guide to less stress and more connection.

Next Up: Why Doodles Are Different

But why do Doodles need a different approach in the first place?

If you've ever wondered why *traditional dog training methods don't seem to work* on your Doodle—or why they act like a *genius one minute and a tornado the next*—you're not alone.

Doodles aren't just another breed. They're a *unique mix of intelligence, energy, and emotional sensitivity*—and that changes everything.

Turn the page to learn why Doodles are different—and why that matters.

Part 1

Understanding Doodles and Why They Need Structure

"Before I followed this blueprint, I was exhausted. Now, my Doodle finally knows how to settle."

— Melissa, Sheepadoodle parent

Chapter 1

Why Doodles are Different

(And Why That Matters)

If You've Ever Thought, "Why Is My Doodle Like This?"—You're Not Alone

Doodles are different.

They're not just another dog breed—they're a carefully crafted mix of intelligence, energy, and emotional sensitivity. While that combination makes for an incredible companion, it can also lead to frustration if you don't understand how to work with their nature instead of against it.

Many new Doodle parents expect their puppy's boundless energy to naturally settle over time. However, research shows that dogs don't "grow out" of behaviors—they grow into the habits that are reinforced daily (*Mendl, Burman, and Paul, 2010*). Without structure, that high energy and intelligence can turn into nonstop jumping, counter-surfing, and demand barking.

> "Dogs do what works."
>
> —Jean Donaldson

And Doodles? They figure out what works fast—for better or for worse.

This chapter will help you understand why your Doodle acts the way they do—and more importantly, why traditional dog training methods often fail them.

The Doodle Parent Reality Check

Many Doodle parents expect a cuddly, easygoing companion—until they realize just how much intelligence and energy they bring into the home. That's exactly what Abeni experienced when she brought home her Aussiedoodle, Koda...

Abeni, a single mom of two active boys, had dreamed of getting a dog for years. When she brought home Koda, her Aussiedoodle, she was ready for playfulness—but not for the level of energy and intelligence packed into her curly-coated tornado of a dog.

"I thought getting a Doodle meant a fluffy, easygoing dog," she admitted. *"But Koda had me rethinking my whole life! Within a week, he figured out how to open my fridge, undo the baby gate, and even turn on my touch-lamp by nudging it."*

Koda wasn't "misbehaving"—he was just desperate for mental engagement. Once Abeni introduced structured training and sniffari walks (slow, scent-driven walks that let your dog explore the world through their nose), Koda started channeling his intelligence into problem-solving tasks instead of household destruction.

Key Takeaway

Doodles are brilliant, but without structure, they'll invent their own entertainment—and you probably won't like it.

The Doodle Blueprint: A Genetics-Driven Operating System

Think of your Doodle as a high-powered computer system.

At their core, every Doodle runs on a Poodle-based "operating system"—highly intelligent, sensitive, and always scanning for patterns. This means they're wired to learn fast, pick up on routines, and react to changes in their environment with surprising precision.

But that's just the foundation.

On top of that Poodle OS, they also have additional "software" from their other breed influences, which determines how they process information, respond to training, and interact with the world around them.

The challenge? If their operating system isn't managed properly, their software can lead to overstimulation, anxiety, or difficulty settling.

Understanding this 'Doodle Operating System' is the first step—the rest of this book will show you how to optimize their programming with the right structure, routines, and daily rhythms that work with their natural wiring instead of against it. Think of it as the ultimate system upgrade for a calmer, more balanced Doodle.

Let's break it down.

The Poodle Foundation: Where It All Starts

No matter their mix, every Doodle inherits core traits from their Poodle lineage:

- **Elite intelligence**—Poodles consistently rank among the top three smartest dog breeds.

- **Quick pattern recognition**—They learn routines (good or bad) fast.

- **Mental stimulation needs**—Without enough engagement, they'll find their own "jobs" (usually ones you don't like).

- **Environmental sensitivity**—Subtle changes in your mood, schedule, or routine affect them deeply.

- **Athletic ability**—Despite their fluffy looks, Poodles were bred for active work.

That single, perfectly timed bark during your video call? That's not random. It's a calculated decision based on what's worked before.

Doodles aren't just smart—they're strategically intelligent.

But their "software"—the breed traits layered on top of this Poodle OS—determines how that intelligence plays out in daily life.

Your Doodle's Breed-Specific "Software"

Depending on their mix, your Doodle also inherits traits from other breeds that shape their daily needs.

Sporting & Retriever Doodles (Goldendoodles, Labradoodles)

The Social Athletes

- Natural enthusiasm for activities

- Strong retrieval instincts

- High social drive
- Always-on mindset

Daily Impact:

- Thrive on retrieve-based games and structured activities.
- Need clear "off switch" training to settle.
- Struggle with self-regulation without guidance.

Herding Breed Doodles (Aussiedoodles, Sheepadoodles)

The Focused Monitors

- Intense focus abilities
- High environmental awareness
- Strong need for a "job"

Daily Impact:

- Excel with task-based engagement like nose work or agility.
- Need mental challenges to prevent boredom-driven behaviors.
- May struggle with over-arousal from movement or excitement.

Working Breed Doodles (Bernedoodles, Saint Berdoodles)

The Gentle Giants

- Natural calmness (once mature)
- Strong bonding tendency
- Later physical and mental maturity

Daily Impact:

- Require patience during development (they mature slowly).
- Thrive with gentle, structured guidance.
- Need space awareness training due to their size.

Companion Breed Doodles (Cavapoos, Cockapoos, Maltipoos)

The Tiny Therapists

- Deeply bonded to their humans

- Highly intuitive and emotionally responsive

- Thrive on companionship and connection

Daily Impact:

- Need short but meaningful engagement—quick bursts of play, training, or interaction.

- Thrive when included in daily activities rather than being left alone.

- May struggle with overstimulation in busy environments—they feel everything.

Case Study: The Doodle Who Did It All (Too Quickly)

One of the first Doodles I ever worked with was a young Bernedoodle named Hank. His parent brought him to ShedFreeStay™, my exclusive Doodle boarding and training program, because he was "too smart for his own good". The moment I met him, I knew exactly what she meant.

Within the first hour, Hank had:

- Solved every puzzle toy in the play area.

- Retrieved and returned every tennis ball like a professional athlete.

- Mastered an entire agility course he'd never seen before.

His parent watched in amazement, then turned to me and said,

"He's the smartest dog I've ever had... and I have no idea what to do with all that intelligence."

This wasn't unusual. I've seen it with thousands of Doodles—dogs who are brilliant, eager, and affectionate but struggle without the right structure.

For Hank, we implemented a structured daily schedule with predictable morning activities, midday mental enrichment puzzles, and a consistent evening wind-down routine. Within just two weeks, his boundless energy transformed into focused engagement, proving that even the most brilliant Doodles thrive when they know exactly what to expect—and when.

Next Up: The Science Behind Why Routines Work

Now that you understand why Doodles are different, the next step is learning how to work with their natural instincts instead of against them.

So what's the secret to a calmer, more focused Doodle?

- It's not just more training.

- It's not just more exercise.

- It's **predictability—the secret ingredient training alone can't replace.**

Turn the page to learn how a well-designed daily schedule can do what training alone can't.

Chapter 2

The Science of a Well-Balanced Doodle

Why Structure Is the Secret to a Calmer, Happier Doodle

Some Dogs Just "Get It"—And Then There Are Doodles

Some dogs seem to naturally go with the flow. They nap while their parents work, transition smoothly between activities, and wait patiently for their afternoon walk.

And then there are Doodles.

Doodles slam into furniture at full speed, demand-bark in your face at 6 p.m., and act like you've committed a crime if you close the bathroom door. They have endless enthusiasm, an incredible ability to read your every move, and an energy level that can go from zero to zoomies in seconds.

They're also *completely* worth it.

But Doodles *don't* come preprogrammed to be easy. Without a structured routine, their energy can feel overwhelming, and their intelligence can work against them. That's why *structure isn't just helpful—it's essential.*

Why "Just Tire Them Out" Doesn't Work

Many Doodle parents, especially those with high-energy adolescents, hear the same advice:

"If your dog is acting up, they just need more exercise."

This advice sounds logical, but it often backfires.

Research on working dogs has shown that physical exercise alone doesn't calm a dog down—it builds their stamina (*Blackwell et al., 2013*). That means the more you exercise them, the more they expect—and the harder they become to tire out.

For Doodles, who are both intelligent and social, mental engagement matters just as much—if not more—than physical activity.

ENGAGEMENT STRATEGY
Instead of relying on exercise alone,
let's compare different strategies:

STRATEGY	OUTCOME
More exercise (long walks, fetch, running)	Builds endurance; dog gets fitter, not calmer.
Sniff walks, puzzle games, problem-solving tasks	Engages brain; promotes faster relaxation.
Structured routine (The Doodle Daily Schedule Blueprint™)	Reduces stress; dog learns when to expect activity & rest.

This is why **The Doodle Daily Schedule Blueprint™** doesn't just focus on exercise—it balances **mental stimulation, rest, and training,** ensuring that your Doodle's energy is directed productively.

© THE DOODLE PROS

Get your full-color printable version inside your Doodle Daily Toolkit™—ready when you are!

Cortisol Regulation and Stress Reduction

Dogs without predictable schedules stay in a constant state of alertness, leading to higher stress levels and more impulsive behavior (*Hiby et al., 2006*).

Further research by Koolhaas et al. (2011) showed that unpredictability is one of the key factors in triggering stress responses in mammals. For Doodles, with their high cognitive abilities, this stress from unpredictability can show up as anxiety or hyperactivity.

Decision Fatigue: Why Less Choice Reduces Stress

Every day, your Doodle makes hundreds of tiny decisions:

- Do I follow my human or go to my bed?

- Do I bark at the noise or ignore it?

- Do I settle down or keep pacing?

When dogs constantly have to guess what's happening next, their brains get exhausted. This is called *decision fatigue*—and just like with people, it leads to reduced impulse control, heightened reactivity, and more demand barking.

A predictable daily schedule removes the guesswork, allowing your Doodle to relax instead of constantly checking in for direction.

Case Study: The Adolescent Doodle Who "Forgot" Her Training

At nine months old, Bella, a Goldendoodle, had been through puppy training and knew all her commands. Her parents, Mark and Lisa, had followed every piece of advice they had received:

- Early socialization

- Basic obedience training

- Plenty of playtime and walks

But as Bella entered adolescence, everything fell apart.
She started ignoring recall cues, stealing food from counters, and barking constantly when left alone—behaviors she had never struggled with before.
Lisa told me:
"It felt like she had forgotten everything we worked on. We thought we were doing something wrong, so we just exercised her more—but that only made things worse."
Bella wasn't being stubborn—she was struggling with impulse control, something adolescent Doodles don't just "grow out of".

The Science of Why Routines Work

What finally helped Bella wasn't more exercise—it was a structured, predictable daily routine that worked with her natural rhythms.

The Magic of Muscle Memory: How Routines Shape Behavior

Have you ever driven home from work and realized you don't remember parts of the drive? Or found yourself reaching for your morning coffee before you're fully awake?

That's your brain's habit system at work.

Back in 1998, Dr. Ann Graybiel at MIT made a fascinating discovery about how habits form.

Think of your brain (and your Doodle's) as having an *autopilot system*. Once you perform an action consistently, this autopilot takes over, turning conscious efforts into automatic responses. This is precisely how habit loops form in both humans and dogs.

This research was later expanded by Duhigg (2012) in his analysis of habit loops, showing how cues and rewards create automatic behavioral responses. For Doodles, establishing these positive habit loops through consistent daily routines *creates automatic 'settling' behaviors instead of constantly seeking stimulation.*

This is why **The Doodle Daily Schedule Blueprint™** works so well.

Once your Doodle learns their daily rhythm, they automatically start to settle when expected, engage when cued, and rest when it's time.

One of my clients, Emma, used to struggle with her Goldendoodle's endless pacing after dinner.

"It's like he can't settle unless I play with him for hours," she told me.

But once we established a simple pattern—dinner, followed by a special chew toy—something magical happened.

Within just three weeks, her Doodle started naturally settling after meals. What began as a 5-minute settle with constant redirection gradually extended to 30 minutes of calm relaxation—all because we created consistent cues and expectations around mealtime.

The dinner became the cue, settling became the behavior, and the chew toy was the reward.

Without clear patterns, your Doodle will create their own habits—and they don't always make the best choices.

The Clear Takeaways
- More exercise does not mean better behavior—in fact, it can make high-energy Doodles even harder to settle.

- Routines reduce decision fatigue, helping Doodles relax instead of staying in a heightened state of alertness.

- Impulse control and mental work matter more than tiring them out.

Bella's story is a perfect example of how *structure—not exhaustion—creates a balanced Doodle.*

This is why **The Doodle Daily Schedule Blueprint™** is at the core of this book—it's the key to preventing overstimulation, reinforcing good habits, and helping your Doodle feel secure in their daily life.

> *"The recipe for success as a puppy parent is patience, consistency, and a predictable schedule. Puppies thrive when they know what's expected of them— and when."*
> Dorothy Sparacino, Owner of and Cavapoo Breeder for Puppy Perfectionist

 **Download Your Free Doodle Daily Toolkit™**

Want help structuring your Doodle's routine? **Download The Doodle Daily Toolkit™ for printable daily schedule templates** at:

thedoodlepro.com/bonustoolkit

What Comes Next: Designing Your Doodle's Ideal Schedule

Now that you understand why structure works, it's time to start designing your Doodle's ideal daily schedule.

In the next chapter, we'll take these *science-backed principles* and create a step-by-step routine that channels their energy, prevents bad habits, and creates a calmer, happier dog.

Now that you understand the 'why' behind Doodle behavior and the science that supports structured routines, you're ready for the 'how.' In the following chapters, we'll move from theory to practical application, giving you specific schedules, routines, and frameworks that put these principles to work. You'll see exactly how to structure your day—from morning to night—to create the consistency your Doodle craves while maintaining the flexibility your life demands.

Turn the page to learn how to design your Doodle's ideal daily schedule—one that transforms chaos into calm and frustration into flow. Let's put these principles into action!

Part 2

The Doodle Daily Schedule Blueprint™

"Once I followed the routine, my Doodle stopped the constant demand barking and actually learned how to settle!"

— Omari, Whoodle parent

Chapter 3

The Doodle Daily Schedule Blueprint™

A Proven Structure for a Calmer, Happier Life

You've tried "winging it." You've tried "wear them out." Now it's time for what actually works.

Is This Chapter for You?

If you're picking up this book, chances are you're looking for a more enjoyable life with your Doodle—not just a way to manage their energy, but a way to create a *balanced, stress-free routine* that works for both of you.

Maybe you want a detailed, hour-by-hour schedule to follow. Or maybe you just need a clear rhythm to reduce chaos and help your Doodle settle.
Good news: you'll get both. Maybe you want a detailed, hour-by-hour schedule. Or maybe you just need a steady rhythm to reduce chaos and help your Doodle settle.

This Blueprint gives you flexible structure without the pressure of the clock—and sample routines for those who want more detail.

Whether you days are consistent or chaotic, it's not about the clock—it's about rhythm. That's where anchor points come in: repeatable moments that give your Doodle structure—even when life doesn't.

Thank: "after breakfast time = potty then mat time," or "after soccer drop-off = scent game + settle."

If your family juggles work shifts or busy weekends, this kind of predictability is key. Anchor points help your doodle stay grounded—even when the schedules shifts.

The **Doodle Daily Schedule Blueprint™** isn't about micromanaging every minute of your day—it's about creating a *repeatable structure* that gives your Doodle the predictability they crave while adapting to your life and routine.

This provides your Doodle a buffer for when things change—and a quick path back to calm when the routine returns.

That's why this system works.

The Complete Blueprint: What Your Doodle Needs Daily

Doodles don't just need *more exercise or more training*—they need the *right balance* of structure and engagement.

This book will show you how to create a *predictable, adaptable daily flow* that prevents behavior problems before they start:

- **The Doodle Morning Flow™** – How to start the day right (calm, not chaotic).

- **The Doodle Midday Reset™** – How to avoid the afternoon slump and destruction.

- **The Doodle Wind-Down Plan™** – How to channel zoomies so they don't knock over Grandma.

- **Potty Training & Crate Comfort Schedules** – How to build lifelong habits.

- **Mental Enrichment Strategies**– Engage your Doodle's brain to prevent boredom-based behavior problems.

- **Real-Life Routine Adjustments** – How to adapt your schedule for travel, workdays, weekends, and unexpected life chaos.

- **Puppy & Adolescent Doodle Schedules** – Stage-specific routines that grow with your dog.

Why You Can Trust This Blueprint: Over 50,000 Hours of Real-World Results

This isn't just another dog training schedule—it's a *Doodle-specific system* built through *real-world experience.*

I didn't create this system based on theory—I built it through 50,000+ *hours working exclusively with Doodles at ShedFreeStay™*, my one-of-a-kind Doodle-only boarding and training program.

Across nearly a decade, I've worked with *thousands of Doodles* of every breed mix, size, and personality. I've tested every training method, exercise routine, and schedule adjustment imaginable to see what actually works—and what fails spectacularly.

I've seen firsthand:

- What happens when Doodles don't have structure (*spoiler: chaos*).
- What happens when parents over-exercise their Doodles, thinking it will "calm them down" (*it doesn't*).
- How a well-designed daily routine can transform an overstimulated, anxious Doodle into a calm, well-adjusted companion—without hours of daily training.

ShedFreeStay™ became my real-world behavioral lab, and after *thousands of overnights*, one undeniable pattern emerged:

When families switched from *reactive chaos to a proactive daily rhythm*, everything changed.

- Doodles stopped demand barking.
- They settled on their own instead of needing constant attention.
- They actually learned how to relax.

That's what this **Blueprint** is designed to do for you.

Why Structure (Not Strictness) Is the Secret to Success

Doodles don't need a rigid schedule, but they do thrive on *predictable rhythms.*

Without a structured day, their intelligence and energy can quickly turn into:

- Destructive behaviors

- Demand barking

- Endless zoomies at the worst possible times

Rather than focusing on the clock, this Blueprint helps you create a *natural flow* to your Doodle's day—one that prevents:

- Morning chaos that leaves you frustrated before your first sip of coffee.

- Midday boredom that leads to destruction.

- Evening zoomies that make relaxing impossible.

Do you work best with a strict schedule? Go for it, I'll provide you samples.

Want more flexibility? Just follow the routine at the times that fit your schedule.

The timing can shift, but *the structure remains the same*—whether your Doodle is a *playful puppy, a testing adolescent, or a settled adult.*

Case Study: From Chaos to Calm—Zeke the Whoodle

Without a predictable routine, Doodles struggle to know *when to engage, rest, or settle.*

This was the challenge Omari and Kiara faced with their Whoodle, Zeke.

Omari and Kiara, a busy couple balancing two full-time careers and twin toddlers, felt like they'd made a huge mistake after adopting Zeke, their playful Whoodle.

"He was adorable, but he was everywhere at once," Kiara said. *"I felt like I had a third toddler—barking, chewing, and bouncing off the walls. I was exhausted."*

Without a structured routine, Zeke never knew *when to expect food, play-time, or rest*—so he stayed in a constant state of overdrive. Once Omari and Kiara implemented the Blueprint, everything shifted.

"It was like magic," Omari said. *"Once Zeke knew when to expect things, he actually started to relax. Now, he naps while we work and waits patiently for playtime instead of demand-barking."*

Key Takeaway

Doodles don't just need exercise—they need *predictable rhythms* to feel secure.

Pro Reality Check: This Blueprint doesn't skip exercise—it helps you balance it. You can still enjoy hikes, beach days, and playtime. But now, you'll know how to reset afterward—and give your Doodle what they really need: predictability, not constant motion. Remember, this schedule is your home base, not your leash.

Let's look at why structure works better than just wearing them out.

The Science Behind Why This Works

Through years of working with Doodles, I've seen one truth proven over and over:

Predictable routines create calm far more effectively than exhaustion ever could.

The Cortisol Connection

Studies show that dogs without clear daily routines maintain higher cortisol (stress hormone) levels throughout the day (*Hiby et al.,* 2006).

When your Doodle doesn't know what to expect next, they stay in a state of constant alertness, wondering:

- When's the next walk?
- Is it time to play?
- Or is it time to sleep?
- Will someone feed me soon?

This uncertainty keeps their *stress system activated*, leading to:

- Hyperactivity
- Difficulty settling
- Increased reactivity
- Poor impulse control

Now That You've Seen the Blueprint, You Might Be Wondering...

- Why does my Doodle need this level of structure in the first place?
- What makes Doodles so different from other dogs?
- Why do they seem to have *endless energy, selective hearing, or a deep need*

to be involved in everything?

Next Up: The Doodle Morning Flow™

Now that you understand **the power of structure** and why the Blueprint works, it's time to dive into how to start the day right.

In the next chapter, we'll break down **The Doodle Morning Flow™**—a simple, effective way to *prevent morning chaos* and set your Doodle (and yourself) up for a successful day. You'll learn how to transform those chaotic mornings into a calm, predictable routine that benefits both you and your Doodle.

Turn the page to learn how to start each day with *calm, focus, and balance.*

Chapter 4

The Doodle Morning Flow™

How to Start the Day Right (Calm, Not Chaotic) for a Peaceful Day

Preventing Morning Chaos: A Step-by-Step Guide to Starting Your Doodle's Day Calmly

If your mornings feel more like a Doodle-powered carnival than a calm start to your day, you're not alone—and this chapter might just change your life.

Is This Chapter for You?

Does your Doodle explode with energy the second they wake up—long before your coffee kicks in?

- Zoom through the house while you're trying to get dressed?

- Demand attention the second your feet hit the floor?

- Bark at you during breakfast or paw at you while you check emails?

- Act like they haven't been fed in days, even though you just gave them breakfast?

If this sounds familiar, you're not alone.

Many Doodle parents tell me their mornings feel like chaos—a race to manage their dog's energy while getting ready for work, kids, or life in general.

The Good News:

A well-structured morning routine is the single biggest game-changer for creating a *calmer, more predictable day* with your Doodle.

In This Chapter, You'll Learn:

- The science behind why mornings feel so chaotic (and how to fix it).

- How to structure your morning so your Doodle starts the day calmly.

- A step-by-step schedule for puppies, adolescents, and adult Doodles.

- Troubleshooting tips if your Doodle struggles to adjust.

Meet Max: The Goldendoodle Who Ran Morning Sprints Around the Couch

When Max's parent, Sarah, called me, she sounded completely drained.
"I don't even get a chance to wake up before Max is bouncing off the walls!"
She described a familiar scene:

- **6:00 a.m.** – Max launched himself off the couch, doing laps around the living room.

- **6:15 a.m.** – He barked at Sarah while she made coffee, jumping up to get her attention.

- **6:30 a.m.** – He devoured his breakfast in ten seconds flat, then immediately started pawing at her for more.

- **6:45 a.m.** – When Sarah sat down to check emails, Max shoved every toy he owned into her lap—one after the other.

- **7:00 a.m.** – By the time she needed to start work, Max was still going—and she was already exhausted.

Sarah had tried everything—longer walks, ignoring him, even waking up earlier. But nothing worked—Max still seemed wired from the moment he woke up.
So, I asked her a simple question:
"What's Max's actual morning structure?"
She paused. *"I guess... I don't really have one? I just try to keep up with him."*
And that was the problem.

Why Mornings Feel Like Chaos (And How to Fix It)

Through years of working with Doodles, I've noticed one universal truth:

If a Doodle starts the day overstimulated, the chaos doesn't just disappear—it builds throughout the day.

That means:

- Morning zoomies turn into midday demand barking.

- Impulse control issues get worse by the afternoon.

- By evening, they're still wired—and bedtime becomes a battle.

Doodles don't just "settle" into the day—they take behavioral cues from their environment.

The key to fixing this cycle? Understanding *why Doodles wake up like tiny tornadoes*—and how to channel that energy before it spirals out of control.

The Science of Morning Overarousal

Ever wonder why your Doodle wakes up like they just had three shots of espresso? It's not just excitement—it's science.

Cortisol Spikes: Why Mornings Start Wired

Just like humans, dogs experience a *natural spike in cortisol* (the stress hormone) when they wake up (*Hiby et al., 2006*).

That means they're *primed to move, explore, and engage*—which explains why they burst into zoomies before you've even had coffee.

Unstructured Mornings Fuel Chaos

Dogs don't like guessing games—they want to know exactly when and how things happen.

Without a *predictable morning flow*, they'll try to fill in the blanks themselves—and trust me, their version of a "morning routine" usually involves barking at you, zooming around the house, or staring at you like you've forgotten your life's purpose.

Hyperactivity Feeds Itself

Here's the thing about hyperactivity—it doesn't burn out; it *builds up*.

If your Doodle starts the day at 100 mph, they don't just get tired and settle—they *get better at staying wired.*

Think of it like giving a toddler candy for breakfast and expecting them to take a nap afterward.

The Fix: The Doodle Morning Flow™

The **Doodle Morning Flow™** helps *regulate wake-up energy*, providing *structure instead of chaos.*

This plan *sets the tone for a calm, structured day* by balancing movement, engagement, and rest.

THE DOODLE MORNING FLOW™:
A STEP-BY-STEP ROUTINE FOR CALM MORNINGS

KEY PRINCIPLES OF A GOOD MORNING ROUTINE

✓ **Potty before play.**	Your Doodle needs to **relieve themselves first**—no distractions, no playtime.
✓ **Start with structure, then excitement.**	After potty break, do a little **light training,** followed by **structured exuberant play to release energy appropriately.**
✓ **Use engagement before food.**	Training or **exercise before breakfast** helps **build impulse control.**
✓ **Teach a settle cue.**	Your Doodle should learn that **after breakfast, it's time to relax.**

© THE DOODLE PROS

Your Bonus Toolkit provides a full-color printable version.

A structured morning routine is essential for setting the tone of the day. Doodles, known for their intelligence and energy, thrive on predictable patterns. Whether you have a young puppy learning the ropes or an adolescent Doodle testing boundaries, a morning schedule that includes movement, mental stimulation, and rest will help prevent chaotic energy bursts later in the day.

Morning Reset (6:00 a.m. – 12:00 p.m.)

Begin the morning with structure, gradually increasing activity.

Start with a *calm potty break and light training,* followed by *structured exuberant play* to release energy in a productive way. Avoid chaotic, unstructured play that ramps up energy too quickly. This period sets the tone for a calm, structured day by balancing movement, engagement, and rest.

MORNING FLOW™
BLUEPRINT

TIME	ACTIVITY	NOTES
6:00AM	Potty Break	Quick, no play outside.
6:15AM	Training or Scent Work	Builds impulse control before breakfast.
6:30AM	Breakfast in a Puzzle Feeder	Slows eating and encourages engagement.
7:00AM	Moderate Walk or Exuberant Play	Maintains physical health and mental balance.
8:00AM	Settle Time- Chew Toy or Mat Training	Teaches relaxation after activity.
9:00AM	Crate or Pen Rest	Promotes calm behavior and independent downtime.
11:00AM	Gentle Potty Break & Light Movement	Prepares for midday engagement.

© THE DOODLE PRO®

Download your printable version inside the Doodle Daily Toolkit™

For puppy-specific adaptations **refer to Chapter 7.**For adolescent routines, head to **Chapter 12**.

Troubleshooting Common Morning Issues

"My Doodle still seems hyper after breakfast!"

- Add a long-lasting chew (bully stick, frozen Kong) right after breakfast to extend calm time.

Pro Tip: For *small Doodles* or those on *calorie-restricted diets*, chews can still be part of your routine—just choose wisely. Try low-calorie options like air-dried fish skins or collagen sticks, or use part of their meal in a frozen Kong, or opt for a food-stuffed toy with their regular kibble. Remember, the *act* of chewing is what helps regulate energy and stress—not the *calories*.

"They demand play first thing in the morning."

- Redirect with engagement-based activities (sniffari, food puzzles, short training) instead of high-energy play.

"They struggle to settle after the morning routine."

- Be consistent—many Doodles take *one to two weeks to adjust.* Stick with it!

Next Up: The Doodle Midday Reset™: Preventing the Afternoon Slump

Now that your morning routine is set, what happens when that *calm energy wears off by noon?*

In the next chapter, we'll cover:

- How to avoid midday chaos.

- Preventing demand barking.

- Creating a structured break that keeps your Doodle balanced.

 **Download The Doodle Daily Toolkit™** for printable morning routines, training resources, and expert-approved schedule guides at:

thedoodlepro.com/bonustoolkit

Turn the page to create a midday routine that keeps the day on track—and your Doodle happy and calm.

Chapter 5

The Doodle Midday Reset™

How to Avoid the Afternoon Slump and Destruction

A **Step-by-Step Guide to Preventing Demand Barking, Restlessness, and Midday Chaos**

Does your Doodle seem like they have two completely different personalities depending on the time of day?

Is This Chapter for You?

Are they:

- Calm and predictable in the morning—but a *demand-barking, zoomie-fueled tornado* by mid-afternoon?

- Settled while you work, then suddenly *whining, pacing, or stealing socks* around lunchtime?

- Peaceful in the crate after breakfast, but by noon, *barking at every sound* and staring at you like they've never been fed?

You're not imagining things. This is normal—and fixable.

Many Doodles experience a *midday energy shift*—a natural spike in activity followed by a struggle to settle down.

In This Chapter, You'll Learn:

- Why this energy surge happens—and how to manage it

- How to structure the middle of the day to prevent overstimulation

- A step-by-step **Midday Reset™ schedule** for puppies, adolescents, and adults

- Troubleshooting tips for common midday struggles

Meet Cooper: The Bernedoodle Who Barked Through Every Zoom Call

Jennifer, a marketing executive working from home, was at her wit's end with her Bernedoodle, Cooper.

"Mornings are fine—he naps while I work. But after lunch, it's like a switch flips."

She described a typical afternoon:

- **12:30 p.m.** – Cooper started pacing and whining while she was on a Zoom call.

- **1:00 p.m.** – If she ignored him, he barked at the window, at his toys, at absolutely nothing.

- **1:30 p.m.** – When that didn't work, he started pawing at her chair and jumping up to steal papers off her desk.

- **2:00 p.m.** – By the time she finished meetings, Cooper was still wired—zooming around the house, chewing furniture, and getting into anything he could find.

Jennifer had tried longer morning walks, interactive toys, even feeding Cooper later—but nothing worked.

What she didn't realize was that Cooper wasn't getting "more energy" midday—he was struggling with overstimulation and a lack of predictable structure.

After implementing **The Doodle Midday Reset™**, *the transformation was immediate.*

"He still has energy, but now he actually settles. It's the first time in months I've had a calm afternoon!"

Why Midday Chaos Happens (and How to Fix It)

Through **50,000+ hours working exclusively with Doodles**, I've seen one truth play out over and over:

- **Morning structure sets the day up for success.**

- **But midday structure keeps that success from unraveling.**

If you don't *proactively manage your Doodle's midday rhythm*, the day naturally spirals into overstimulation, demand barking, or hyperactivity.

If your Doodle barks, paces, or seems restless every afternoon, they're not misbehaving—they're *looking for engagement*. Alejandra learned this the hard way with her Sheepadoodle, Bruno...

Bruno's Midday Barking Problem (and the Simple Fix That Worked)

Alejandra, a freelance graphic designer, loved working from home—until she got Bruno.

"I could *handle deadlines and client calls, but I was not prepared for Bruno barking every time I sat down,*" she said. "*He'd nap peacefully all morning, then suddenly, around lunchtime, he'd start barking non-stop at... nothing!*"

Bruno wasn't misbehaving—he was experiencing a natural midday energy spike. His body was ready for engagement, but he had no idea what to do with himself.

By adding a structured **Midday Reset™**—a sniff walk followed by puzzle feeding—Bruno's barking completely disappeared within a week.

"*Now, he gets his needs met at the right time and spends the afternoon quietly snoozing next to me while I work,*" Alejandra said.

Key Takeaway

Doodles need a structured midday routine—*ignoring this window leads to demand barking and restlessness.*

The Science Behind the Midday Slump

The Natural Energy Dip

Research shows that dogs experience a biological energy fluctuation around midday (*Hiby et al., 2006*).

If they don't have a structured routine during this time, they may start pacing, whining, or barking simply because they don't know what to do next.

Morning Engagement Fades—But They Haven't Settled Yet

Even if your Doodle had a structured morning, by noon, their mental and physical energy may be out of sync.

Instead of settling into a calm afternoon, they ping-pong between restlessness and demand behaviors.

Decision Fatigue Peaks

Every hour, your Doodle makes *hundreds of tiny choices:*

- *Do I follow my human or go to my bed?*

- *Do I bark at the noise or ignore it?*

- *Do I settle down or keep pacing?*

By midday, this mental fatigue makes impulse control harder—leading to *worse behavior.*

The Solution? A **predictable Midday Reset™** that channels energy correctly while reinforcing calm behaviors.

The Doodle Midday Reset™: A Step-by-Step Routine for Balanced Afternoons

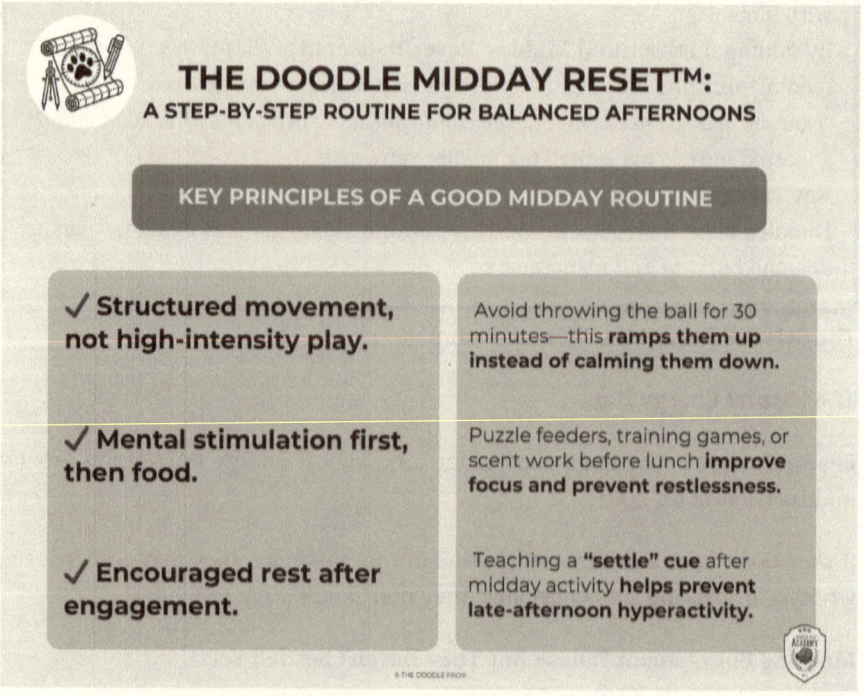

THE DOODLE MIDDAY RESET™:
A STEP-BY-STEP ROUTINE FOR BALANCED AFTERNOONS

KEY PRINCIPLES OF A GOOD MIDDAY ROUTINE

✓ **Structured movement, not high-intensity play.**	Avoid throwing the ball for 30 minutes—this **ramps them up instead of calming them down.**
✓ **Mental stimulation first, then food.**	Puzzle feeders, training games, or scent work before lunch **improve focus and prevent restlessness.**
✓ **Encouraged rest after engagement.**	Teaching a **"settle" cue** after midday activity **helps prevent late-afternoon hyperactivity.**

© THE DOODLE FROM

For Puppy adaptations, see Chapter 7. For adolescent Doodles, go to Chapter 12.

This period focuses on *structured engagement, meals, and rest* to set up a smooth afternoon.

MIDDAY RESET BLUEPRINT™

TIME	ACTIVITY	NOTES
12:00PM	Potty Break & Structured Movement	Quick, no play outside.
12:15PM	Training or Scent Work	Short, engaging mental exercise.
12:30PM	Lunch in a Puzzle Feeder	Slows eating and keeps them engaged.
12:45PM	Crate or Pen rest	Prevents overtired zoomies later.
2:00PM	Gentle Potty Break & Movement	No high-energy play.
2:30PM	Calm Socialization or Chew Time	Exposure to new sights/sounds in a relaxed manner.
3:00PM	Afternoon Nap in Crate or Room	Helps maintain energy balance for a calmer evening.

© THE DOODLE PRO®

Full-color printable version is waiting in your Toolkit!

Adapting the Reset for Lunch Breaks or Dog Walkers:

- **If hiring a dog walker:** A structured leash walk can replace midday training or scent work, but keep it calm—*no intense play or fetch.*

- **If coming home for lunch:** Prioritize a *calm potty break first*—no high-energy play.

- Provide **mental enrichment** like a snuffle mat, frozen Kong, or a quick 2-3 minute training game.

- Reinforce **settling behaviors** before you or the walker leave again, using a chew toy or place training.

For *slow feeder recommendations*, access *reader-exclusive discounts* on my favorites in your Doodle Daily Toolkit™.

Troubleshooting Common Midday Issues

"My Doodle still gets the zoomies after lunch!"

- Shift their midday enrichment to *pre-lunch* so they can settle afterward.

"They bark at me while I work!"

- Introduce *clear engagement times* so they learn when to expect attention.

"They won't rest after activity!"

- Stick with it—most Doodles need 1-2 weeks to adjust to the new rhythm.

Next Up: The Doodle Wind-Down Plan™: Ending the Day on a Calm Note

Now that your midday routine is in place, what happens when the evening energy kicks in?

In the next chapter, we'll cover:

- Why Doodles get sudden bursts of energy at night—even after a structured day.

- How to prevent bedtime zoomies, demand barking, and restlessness.

- The best way to wind down your Doodle so they settle easily.

 **Download The Doodle Daily Toolkit™** for printable **midday routines, training resources, schedule guides, and reader-exclusive discounts** at:

thedoodlepro.com/bonustoolkit

Turn the page to set up an evening routine that helps your Doodle (and you) get a peaceful night's rest.

Chapter 6

The Doodle Evening Blueprint™

Witching Hour and Wind-Down Strategies

E venings with a Doodle can feel like *the calm before the storm—or just the storm itself.*

Is This Chapter for You?

Does your Doodle:

- Suddenly explode with energy right before bed?

- Start *demand barking, mouthing, or stealing objects* in an attempt to keep the night going?

- Struggle to settle down, even when the household is winding down for the night?

Evening energy spikes are *predictable, not random.*

In This Chapter, You'll Learn:

- How to prevent overstimulation and zoomies at the worst times.

- How to create a predictable bedtime routine that helps your Doodle relax.

- How to make evenings calmer—for both you and your dog.

Toolkit Reminder: A printable **Evening Wind-Down Routine** is included in **The Doodle Daily Toolkit™**. If you haven't grabbed your Toolkit yet, visit **thedoodlepro.com/bonustoolkit**.

Why Evenings Feel Like Chaos (And How to Fix It)

After working with Doodles for nearly a decade and managing **thousands of overnights** at my **Doodle-only training and boarding program**, I've fine-tuned a rhythm that sets them up for success.

Away from home and their families, I had to crack the code—*finding the secret sauce that transformed restless, overstimulated Doodles into calm, content companions.*

What I uncovered applies just as much in their homes as it does in my boarding program:

If a Doodle doesn't have a structured evening routine, they'll invent their own—and trust me, their version is pure chaos.

That means:

- Pacing and panting instead of settling

- Dropping toys in your lap in a desperate bid for entertainment

- Demand barking when you finally sit down

- Getting into mischief—stealing socks, counter-surfing, or chewing furniture—just to create their own fun

The **Doodle Evening Wind-Down Blueprint™** provides the *right kind of evening activity—engaging their brain *without overstimulating their body.*

Implementing this structure has *transformed restless, overstimulated Doodles into calm, content companions.*

Recognizing Overstimulation Before It Escalates

Dog training isn't just about what you say—it's about what your Doodle is telling you.

Understanding *subtle body language cues* can help *prevent overstimulation*, manage transitions, and reinforce calm behavior *before excitement spirals into chaos*.

> "By observing and interpreting canine body language, parents can prevent stress and behavioral issues before they escalate. Dogs communicate constantly, and subtle cues—like lip licking, yawning, or turning away—are often early signs of discomfort or overstimulation."
> — says Lisa Lyle Waggoner, guest on The Doodle Pro® Podcast

Many Doodle parents *misinterpret these signals or miss them entirely*, leading to situations where a dog **suddenly seems to "explode" into zoomies, demand barking, or mouthing.**

The reality? *Doodles don't go from calm to chaos in an instant*—they communicate their *growing tension long before it escalates.*

Key Signs Your Doodle Is Overstimulated (Before Zoomies or Barking Start)

- **Lip licking or yawning**—Early signs of stress, especially if no food or sleep is involved

- **Turning away or avoiding eye contact**—A subtle way of disengaging

- **Body stiffening or freezing momentarily**—Indicates uncertainty or overstimulation

- **Panting (when not hot or exercised)**—A physiological sign of stress

---

By recognizing these early signals, you can **adjust the environment before your Doodle escalates into hyperactivity or frustration.**

THE DOODLE EVENING WIND-DOWN™:
A STEP-BY-STEP ROUTINE FOR CALM EVENINGS

KEY PRINCIPLES OF A GOOD EVENING ROUTINE

✓ **End high energy play early in the evening**

Structured activities include a **leash walk, controlled fetch with breaks, or tug with release cues**

✓ **Encourage chewing or licking activities.**

A frozen **Kong, lick mat, or chew toy** promotes **relaxation** and helps release excess energy.

✓ **Use soft lighting and a calm environment.**

Dim the lights and lower household noise to **signal that bedtime is approaching.**

✓ **Cue relaxation with a consistent routine.**

Use the **same order of activities** each night, such as a short walk, then chewing time, then settling on their bed.

✓ **Avoid last-minute excitement.**

Keep interactions low-energy **in the hour before bed** to help them shift into a restful state.

© THE DOODLE PRO®

Evening Wind-Down (3:00 p.m. – 9:00 p.m.)

Exuberant play in the evening should be structured and not too close to bedtime. Avoid roughhousing, intense wrestling, or unstructured chasing games that can lead to overstimulation. Instead, focus on activities like a *leash walk, controlled fetch with breaks, or tug with release cues* before transitioning into wind-down activities.

When roughhousing is beneficial:
Roughhousing can be a great way to burn energy and build a bond, but it should be structured. Set clear boundaries (e.g., stop on cue, no jumping or mouthing humans) and use it *only during designated high-energy play windows*, like the **morning (7:00 a.m. - 7:30 a.m.) or the Witching Hour (3:30 p.m. - 5:00 p.m.).**

Evening is often the trickiest time of day—when Doodles are most likely to experience:

- Zoomies

- Nipping

- Frustration behaviors

The *Doodle Daily Schedule Blueprint™* helps guide this time with intentional activities and a structured wind-down.

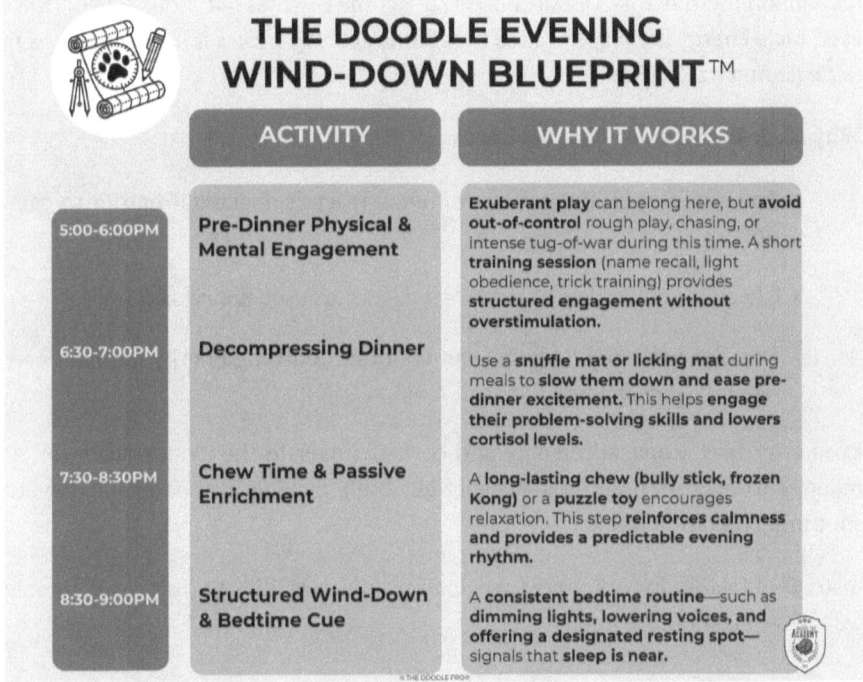

THE DOODLE EVENING WIND-DOWN BLUEPRINT™

	ACTIVITY	WHY IT WORKS
5:00-6:00PM	Pre-Dinner Physical & Mental Engagement	**Exuberant play** can belong here, but **avoid out-of-control** rough play, chasing, or intense tug-of-war during this time. A short **training session** (name recall, light obedience, trick training) provides **structured engagement without overstimulation.**
6:30-7:00PM	Decompressing Dinner	Use a **snuffle mat or licking mat** during meals to **slow them down and ease pre-dinner excitement.** This helps **engage their problem-solving skills and lowers cortisol levels.**
7:30-8:30PM	Chew Time & Passive Enrichment	A long-lasting chew (bully stick, frozen Kong) or a **puzzle toy** encourages relaxation. This step **reinforces calmness and provides a predictable evening rhythm.**
8:30-9:00PM	Structured Wind-Down & Bedtime Cue	A consistent bedtime routine—such as **dimming lights, lowering voices, and offering a designated resting spot—** signals that **sleep is near.**

Your printable version is ready in the Doodle Daily Toolkit™

For **puppy adaptations, see to Chapter 7. For adolescent adjustments, refer to Chapter 12.**

This *structured plan* helps *regulate energy levels before bed* using *calm, predictable activities* instead of high-energy play.

> Whether you work swing shifts, rotate between hybrid days, or chase soccer games on the weekends, your Doodle can still find calm through *anchor points.*
>
> These mini-patterns help your dog know what to expect—even if your schedule looks different every day.

The Science Behind It: Cortisol, Adrenaline, and Evening Hyperactivity

A common myth is that Doodles need to *"get the zoomies out"* before bed. However, *high-energy activity too close to bedtime actually makes it harder for dogs to settle (Horowitz, 2016).*

Why High-Excitement Play Backfires

- Too much excitement *raises adrenaline levels,* making it harder to calm down.

- Chasing, rough play, or running *triggers arousal, not relaxation.*

- Doodles with high stamina can continue "burning energy" *without ever reaching a calm state.*

Even after play stops, adrenaline and cortisol linger in the bloodstream for 30 minutes to over an hour *(McGreevy et al., 2018),* making it difficult for dogs to shift into relaxation mode.

Instead of *fueling hyperactivity,* use *low-arousal activities* to help your Doodle wind down just before bed.

Next Up: Customizing The Blueprint for Every Life Stage

Now the evenings are calm, how do you keep that success going all day long?

Whether you're raising an *energetic 8-week-old or a growing adolescent,* the right schedule makes all the difference.

In the next chapter, we'll build a **step-by-step daily rhythm** that supports your puppy's development and **prevents common struggles before they start.**

Turn the page to discover how to support your puppy's development with structure that grows with them.

Part 3:

Core Puppy Training Essentials

"Structure builds confidence. When puppies know what to expect, they thrive."

—The Doodle Pro®

Chapter 7

The Puppy's Daily Schedule

(8 Weeks - 6 Months)

A **Step-by-Step Guide to Building Early Structure and Preventing Chaos**

If your adorable new Doodle is running on chaos and catnaps—and you're running on caffeine and hope—you're in the right place.

Is This Chapter for You?

Bringing home a Doodle puppy is *equal parts joy and exhaustion.*

You imagined cozy snuggles... but instead, you're up at 3 a.m. for yet another potty break.

Your puppy is either attacking shoelaces like a land shark—or passed out cold.

You've heard so many opinions on training and socialization that it's overwhelming.

You're starting to wonder if Doodle puppies ever actually sleep (*spoiler: they do, but probably not on your schedule—yet*).

If you're reading this with dark circles under your eyes, know this: You are not alone.

Every Doodle parent goes through this phase, and the key to moving from survival mode to success is building a structured daily rhythm from the start.

A structured routine is more than just convenience—it's the key to raising a well-adjusted, confident puppy.

The **Doodle Daily Schedule Blueprint™** is designed to take the guesswork out of puppyhood and give you a predictable, repeatable rhythm that works.

In This Chapter, You'll Learn:

- Why *structure is essential* for puppies—and why "just tiring them out" doesn't work

- How to align your puppy's schedule with **The Doodle Daily Schedule Blueprint™**

- A step-by-step daily routine that prevents overstimulation, accidents, and frustration

- How to adjust your puppy's routine as they grow

Why Structure Is Essential for Your Puppy

New puppy parents hear a lot of *conflicting advice:*

"Just take them out all the time." "They'll figure it out eventually." "Tire them out, and they'll sleep better."

Here's the Truth:

Puppies don't need *exhaustion*—they need *predictability.*

Without a *clear eat, potty, play, sleep cycle,* puppies stay in a *heightened state of excitement,* leading to:

- More accidents

- Overstimulation

- Difficulty settling down

The **Doodle Daily Schedule Blueprint™** ensures they get the *right balance* of activity, engagement, and rest so they can develop *impulse control, self-regulation, and confidence.*

Puppies thrive when they *know what's coming next. Structure builds confidence, prevents overexcitement, and makes housetraining smoother.*

Without a *structured rhythm*, puppies struggle to relax, leading to:

- More accidents

- Demand barking

- Increased frustration

> "Consistency is the key to training your new puppy. Raising a puppy is much like caring for a toddler—routine builds confidence and sets the foundation for lifelong learning. By reinforcing good behavior with praise, you help them grow into a happy, well-adjusted companion."
> —Cindy Boling, Honeysuckle Creek GoldenDoodles

The Puppy Starter Schedule: A Step-by-Step Blueprint

The **Doodle Daily Schedule Blueprint™** applies to all ages, but *puppies need modifications* to fit their developmental needs.

Key Differences Between the Puppy Schedule and the Adult Schedule:

- **More frequent potty breaks.** Young puppies can't hold their bladder for long.

- **Shorter activity sessions.** Their attention span is limited, and they tire quickly.

- **More naps** (*even when they don't think they need them*). Overtired puppies = wild puppies.

- **Extra focus on socialization.** This critical period shapes their future confidence.

"Early socialization—done thoughtfully and safely—prevents fear, builds trust, and lays the foundation for a dog who can handle life with resilience."

—Jane Messineo Lindquist, Creator of Puppy Culture

Morning Routine (6:00 a.m. – 12:00 p.)

Your morning *sets the tone for the entire day.* If it starts chaotic, expect the rest of the day to follow.

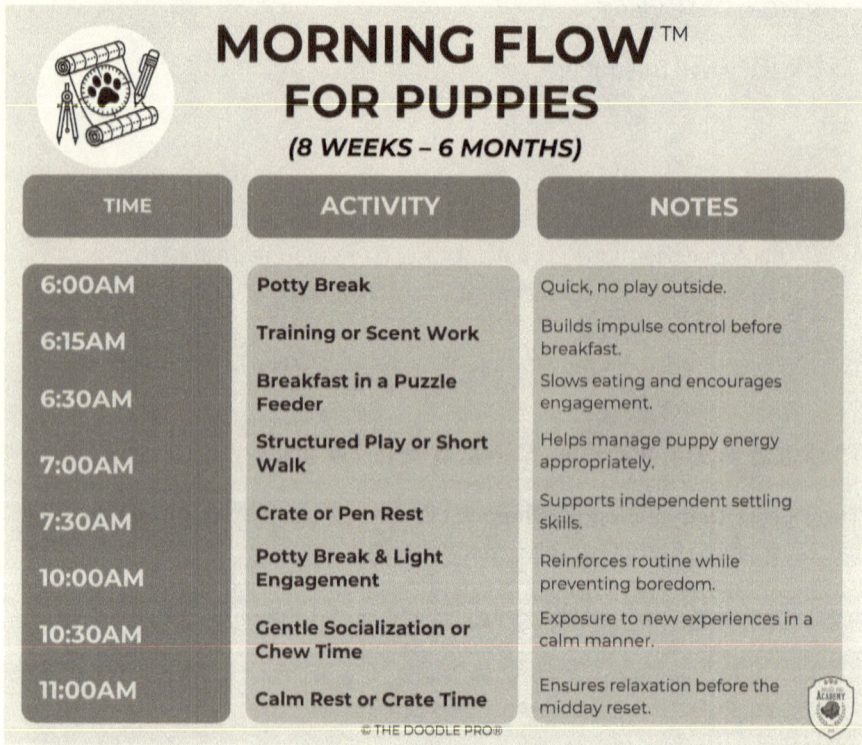

MORNING FLOW™
FOR PUPPIES
(8 WEEKS – 6 MONTHS)

TIME	ACTIVITY	NOTES
6:00AM	Potty Break	Quick, no play outside.
6:15AM	Training or Scent Work	Builds impulse control before breakfast.
6:30AM	Breakfast in a Puzzle Feeder	Slows eating and encourages engagement.
7:00AM	Structured Play or Short Walk	Helps manage puppy energy appropriately.
7:30AM	Crate or Pen Rest	Supports independent settling skills.
10:00AM	Potty Break & Light Engagement	Reinforces routine while preventing boredom.
10:30AM	Gentle Socialization or Chew Time	Exposure to new experiences in a calm manner.
11:00AM	Calm Rest or Crate Time	Ensures relaxation before the midday reset.

© THE DOODLE PRO®

A printable version for the fridge is in your Toolkit. I know you're not getting enough sleep to remember this!

The **Doodle Daily Schedule Blueprint™** recommends a *balance* of potty breaks, meals, structured play, and naps to ensure a *predictable and stress-free morning.*

Midday Routine (12:00 p.m. – 4:00 p.m.)

Midday is the sweet spot for low-key engagement, social exposure, and quality naps.

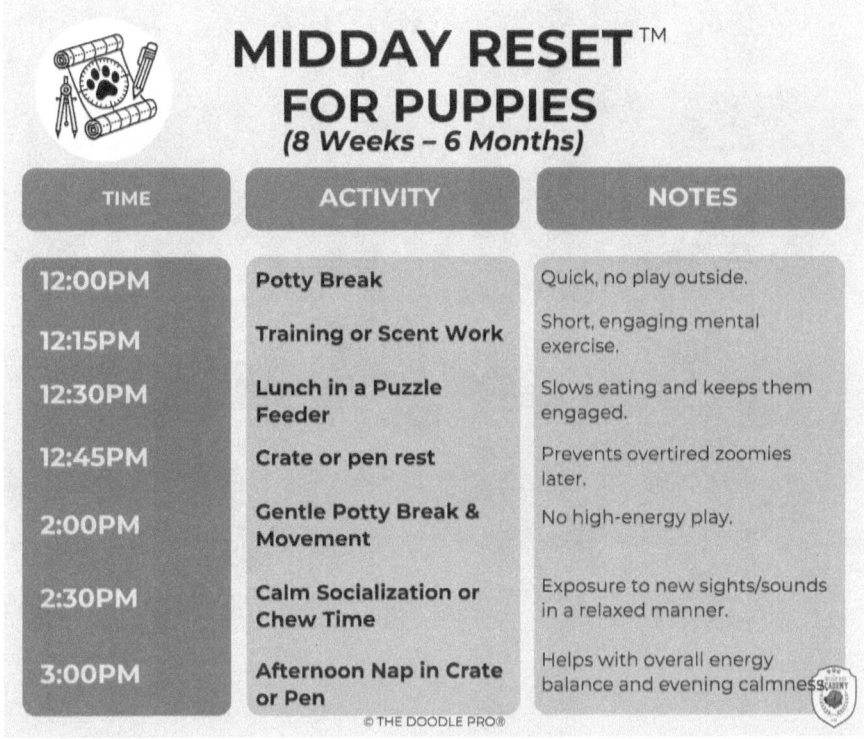

MIDDAY RESET™ FOR PUPPIES
(8 Weeks – 6 Months)

TIME	ACTIVITY	NOTES
12:00PM	Potty Break	Quick, no play outside.
12:15PM	Training or Scent Work	Short, engaging mental exercise.
12:30PM	Lunch in a Puzzle Feeder	Slows eating and keeps them engaged.
12:45PM	Crate or pen rest	Prevents overtired zoomies later.
2:00PM	Gentle Potty Break & Movement	No high-energy play.
2:30PM	Calm Socialization or Chew Time	Exposure to new sights/sounds in a relaxed manner.
3:00PM	Afternoon Nap in Crate or Pen	Helps with overall energy balance and evening calmness

© THE DOODLE PRO®

The **Doodle Daily Schedule Blueprint™** prioritizes *calm, structured activities that reinforce good habits and prevent overstimulation.*

Afternoon & Evening Routine (3:00 p.m. – 7:00 p.m.)

This is the *trickiest time of day*—when puppies are most likely to experience:

- Zoomies

- Nipping

- Frustration behaviors

The **Doodle Daily Schedule Blueprint™** helps guide this time with *intentional activities* and a *structured wind-down*.

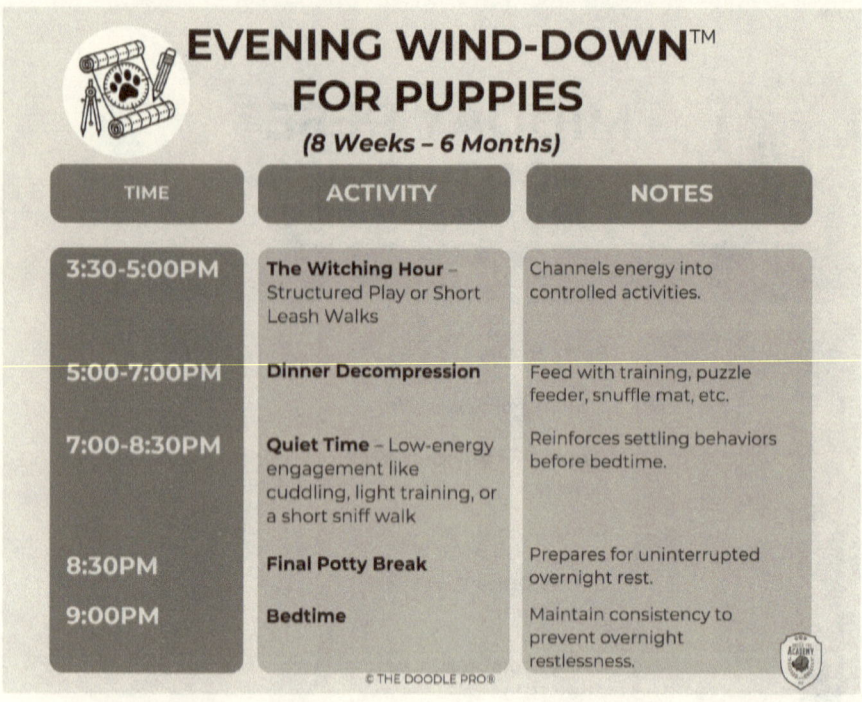

EVENING WIND-DOWN™ FOR PUPPIES
(8 Weeks – 6 Months)

TIME	ACTIVITY	NOTES
3:30-5:00PM	**The Witching Hour** – Structured Play or Short Leash Walks	Channels energy into controlled activities.
5:00-7:00PM	**Dinner Decompression**	Feed with training, puzzle feeder, snuffle mat, etc.
7:00-8:30PM	**Quiet Time** – Low-energy engagement like cuddling, light training, or a short sniff walk	Reinforces settling behaviors before bedtime.
8:30PM	**Final Potty Break**	Prepares for uninterrupted overnight rest.
9:00PM	**Bedtime**	Maintain consistency to prevent overnight restlessness.

© THE DOODLE PRO®

Next Up: Housetraining & Crate Training

Your puppy's routine is getting smoother—but what about those accidents?

If you're dealing with accidents, confusion, or inconsistent progress, you're not alone.

In the next chapter, we'll break down the most effective potty training system—so your puppy learns faster, and you can ditch the constant cleanups.

Turn the page for step-by-step potty training success—so you can ditch the mop and reclaim your sanity.

Chapter 8

Potty Training Puppies

Setting the Foundation for Success

If it feels like you're stuck on endless potty patrol, this chapter is your roadmap to relief.

A Step-by-Step Guide to Building Habits and Preventing Accidents

Is This Chapter for You?

Potty training is one of the *biggest concerns* for new Doodle parents—and one of the areas where *small mistakes lead to big frustrations.*

Have you followed all the advice, yet accidents still happen?

Is your puppy doing well one day—then having constant accidents the next?

Do they have no predictable potty schedule, making it impossible to anticipate?

Do they seem determined to test every boundary of potty training?

If any of this sounds familiar, **you're not alone**.

Potty training isn't just about frequency—it's about timing, structure, and teaching your puppy what to expect.

In This Chapter, We'll Break Down:

- A **step-by-step potty training schedule** to prevent accidents before they

happen

- Why **giving too much freedom too soon** can derail progress

- The role of **supervision, consistency, and routine** in setting up success

- How to **troubleshoot common potty training mistakes**

- How long your puppy can **realistically hold it** based on their age

- How potty training fits into **The Doodle Daily Schedule Blueprint™**

Why Potty Training Setbacks Happen—and How to Prevent Them

Many new Doodle parents assume that if their puppy has a *few accident-free days,* they're fully trained.

Then week three hits, and suddenly, *accidents are happening again.*

Here's Why:

- Puppies don't *fully develop bladder control until 5-6 months old—even if* they seem potty trained early on.

- Without a *structured schedule,* puppies forget patterns quickly—*consistency is what makes training stick.*

- *Too much freedom too soon* leads to accidents in hidden spots.

The Most Common Potty Training Mistakes

1. Too Much Freedom Too Soon

It's easy to assume that if your puppy is mostly potty trained, they're ready for *more independence.*

But *too much space, too soon,* is one of the biggest reasons for setbacks.

Why? Puppies don't naturally understand the difference between your living room, bedroom, and backyard. If they suddenly have free rein of the house, they'll pick a quiet, hidden spot to go.

Signs Your Puppy Has Too Much Unsupervised Space:

- Accidents happening behind furniture.

- Accidents near the back door.

- Accidents in a spare bedroom.

What to Do Instead:

Use baby gates or playpens to limit access to just one or two rooms. Expand their freedom gradually—not all at once.

2. Assuming a Puppy is Fully Trained Too Early

Many Doodles seem potty trained around 12-14 *weeks*, only to start having accidents again a few weeks later.

This is normal.

Young puppies don't have *full bladder control* until at least *five to six months old*.

What to Do Instead:

- Stick with *structured potty breaks* even after early success.

- Stay proactive—don't assume they'll *"ask"* to go out every time.

3. Not Supervising Closely Enough

If your puppy has an accident, you didn't just *miss a potty break*—you likely missed *the signals leading up to it.*

Common Signs Your Puppy Needs to Go:

- Sniffing or circling.

- Pausing play suddenly and looking restless.

- Wandering toward a previous accident spot.

If you see any of these signs—*take them outside immediately!*

Many Doodle parents feel *a wave of relief* when their puppy goes several days accident-free—only to be blindsided when accidents suddenly return.

This was exactly what happened to **Farhan and Noor with their Schnoodle, Milo...**

Milo's Potty Training Regression (and How They Fixed It)

Farhan and Noor were thrilled when their 14-*week-old Schnoodle, Milo,* went five days in a row with no accidents.

"*We thought we were done with potty training,*" Noor said.

Then, week three hit. Suddenly, Milo was *peeing inside again—right after he had just gone outside!*

"*At first, we thought he was mad at us,*" Farhan joked. "*Then we realized, he's not being stubborn. He's just a baby who needs structure.*"

Like many puppy parents, they had mistaken early success for full training. By reintroducing stricter supervision and predictable potty breaks, they quickly got Milo back on track.

Key Takeaway

Potty training regression is normal—sticking to structured breaks is the key to long-term success.

The Housetraining Blueprint: A Step-by-Step Daily Schedule

A predictable schedule is the foundation of successful potty training.

The **Doodle Daily Schedule Blueprint™** helps reinforce *when* to eat, *play, rest—and go potty.*

Note: If you've already reviewed the **Puppy Daily Schedule** in **Chapter 7**, you'll see some overlap—because successful potty training depends on consistency.

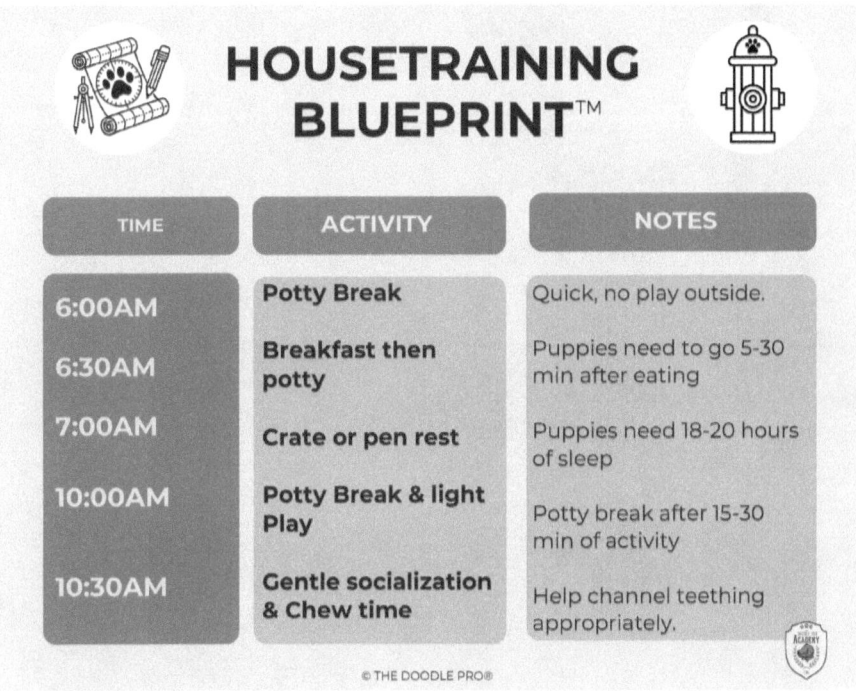

HOUSETRAINING BLUEPRINT™

TIME	ACTIVITY	NOTES
6:00AM	**Potty Break**	Quick, no play outside.
6:30AM	**Breakfast then potty**	Puppies need to go 5-30 min after eating
7:00AM	**Crate or pen rest**	Puppies need 18-20 hours of sleep
10:00AM	**Potty Break & light Play**	Potty break after 15-30 min of activity
10:30AM	**Gentle socialization & Chew time**	Help channel teething appropriately.

© THE DOODLE PRO®

Grab your Housetraining Log from your Doodle Daily Toolkit™ at thedoodlepro.com/bonustoolkit or scan the QR code above.

Next Up: Crate Training & Schedules

You're making progress with potty training—but what about the crate?

A well-introduced crate isn't just for *house training*—it's a *lifelong tool for security, relaxation, and preventing separation stress.*

In the next chapter, we'll cover:

- How to build crate confidence step by step.

- The best way to prevent crate anxiety.

- How to transition to longer crate durations without setbacks.

Turn the page to learn how to make crate training easy, stress-free, and something your puppy actually

Chapter 9

Crate Training and Schedules

Teaching Your Doodle to Love Their Crate

A Step-by-Step Guide to Building Crate Confidence Without Stress

I f you feel guilty using a crate—and your Doodle doesn't seem to love it either—you're not alone. This chapter will show you how to turn it into a place they actually enjoy.

Is This Chapter for You?

Crate training is one of the most *valuable skills* you can teach your Doodle—not just for *puppyhood, but for life.*

- Do they whine or bark in the crate?

- Do they struggle when you leave, even for short periods?

- Do they hesitate to go in, even when it seems comfortable?

This chapter will show you how to turn the crate into a place your Doodle genuinely enjoys.

The goal is for your Doodle to see their crate as a safe, relaxing space—not a place of punishment or isolation.

In This Chapter, You'll Learn:

- How to introduce the crate properly using methods from **Jean Donaldson's, Susan Garrett's Crate Games** and **Malena DeMartini-Price's work on separation anxiety.**

- Why crate training is about providing a structured, secure environment—not confinement.

- How *crate time integrates seamlessly* into **The Doodle Daily Schedule Blueprint™** for a balanced day.

- How to build up alone-time confidence without causing distress.

- The best crate training schedules for different puppy ages.

- How to transition from frequent crate time to more freedom as your Doodle matures.

- Why crate training accelerates house training by creating predictable potty habits.

Why Crate Training Matters (for Life, Not Just Puppyhood)

Many Doodle parents assume that crates are only useful for house training, but a well-trained Doodle will benefit from crate comfort for *years to come.*

A structured daily routine includes crate time not just as a tool for potty training, but as a consistent part of their rhythm for rest, relaxation, and impulse control.

Crates Support Calmness & Adaptability

- **Security During Vet Visits, Grooming, and Boarding** – A Doodle who already sees the crate as a safe space will experience far less stress in these situations.

- **Emergency Preparedness** – Whether for medical recovery, travel, or evacuations, a crate-trained Doodle will have an easier time adjusting.

- **Overstimulation Prevention** – Doodles are prone to self-regulation struggles, and the crate provides a structured way to encourage rest throughout the day.

Most importantly, crate training accelerates house training success by reinforcing natural instincts to keep sleeping areas clean, helping establish consistent potty habits.

> "Crate training helps with housetraining: prompts the dog to hold bladder and bowels when unsupervised to expedite housetraining."
> - Jean Donaldson, Confinement and Crate Training article

This underscores how *strategic crate use within* **The Doodle Daily Schedule Blueprint™** can *reduce accidents and make house training more predictable.*

The goal isn't to phase out crate use entirely—it's to ensure your Doodle always feels secure in it.

Introducing the Crate: Making It a Place They Love

Crate training should be *gradual and positive,* focusing on *building comfort and trust* rather than *forcing confinement.*

Step 1: Build a Positive Association

- Feed meals inside the crate to help your Doodle associate it with something enjoyable.

- Provide high-value chews or puzzle toys only in the crate to create an incentive for them to go in voluntarily.

- Leave the crate door open and encourage relaxed exploration—no pressure.

Step 2: Start With Short, Successful Sessions

- Encouraging short crate stays while you're home ensures the crate doesn't always predict separation.

- Rewarding calm behavior rather than whining or barking reinforces the right habits.

> "Turn crate training into a fun and rewarding experience by making the crate a gateway to great things."
>
> —Susan Garrett, Crate Games

If Your Doodle Resists or Panics in the Crate

Some Doodles experience *separation or confinement anxiety*, which requires a *different approach*.

Signs of Distress Include:

- Excessive drooling

- Trying to escape

- Nonstop, high-pitched barking

What to Do Instead:

- *Take a pause* from crate training and transition to a *playpen setup with the crate inside and the door open.*

- Start with short sessions. Reward calm behavior immediately and consistently.

- Check out **Malena DeMartini's separation anxiety course *Mission Possible*** (*find a reader exclusive discount inside The Doodle Daily Toolkit™*).

- For expert crate training advice, listen to my **interview with Malena DeMartini-Price** on crate training on episode #75 of The Doodle Pro Podcast.

How Long Can Puppies Be in a Crate?

Crate time should align with **The Doodle Daily Schedule Blueprint™**, reinforcing *predictable potty breaks, meals, play, and rest.*

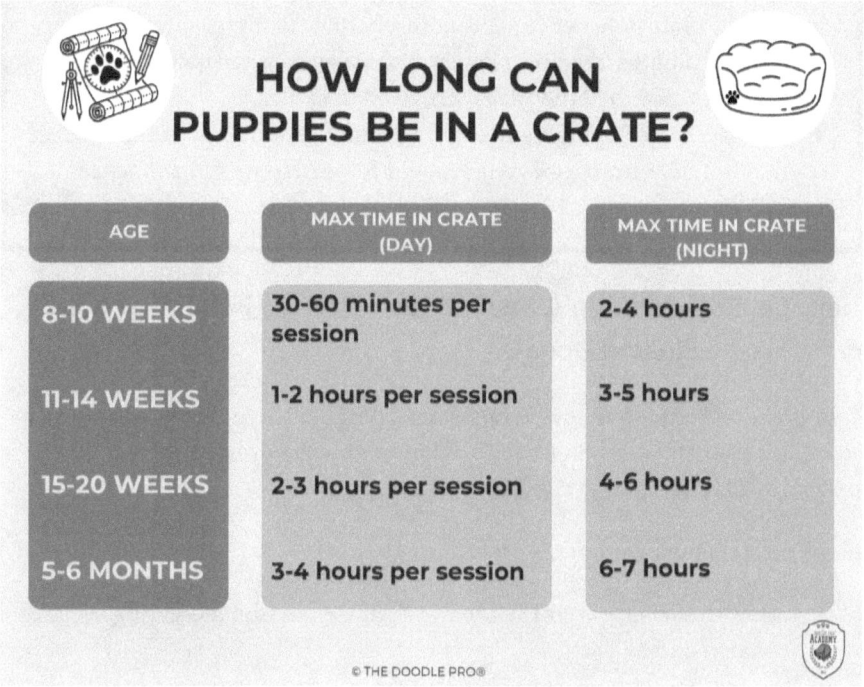

AGE	MAX TIME IN CRATE (DAY)	MAX TIME IN CRATE (NIGHT)
8-10 WEEKS	30-60 minutes per session	2-4 hours
11-14 WEEKS	1-2 hours per session	3-5 hours
15-20 WEEKS	2-3 hours per session	4-6 hours
5-6 MONTHS	3-4 hours per session	6-7 hours

© THE DOODLE PRO®

Note: Puppies *under four months old* may need *one or two nighttime potty breaks.* Keep interactions calm—*potty, then right back to bed.*

Case Study: Why Crate Training Matters

Meet Sarah & Bailey—A Real-Life Crate Training Success Story

When Sarah adopted Bailey, a 10-*week-old Goldendoodle*, she wasn't sure if *crate training was necessary.*

At first, Sarah let Bailey sleep on a dog bed—but within a few weeks, the *overnight accidents started.* Just as Sarah would start to drift off, Bailey *struggled to settle* and repeatedly sought attention, often *waking her up in the middle of the night.*

The Transformation

After Sarah introduced structured crate training using The Doodle Daily Schedule Blueprint™, Bailey began sleeping through the night without accidents. The crate gave her consistent rest periods that prevented overstimulation—and months later, on a family trip, Bailey adjusted quickly thanks to that routine, while the other dogs struggled to settle.

Sarah's experience highlights how *crate training not only accelerates house training* but also prepares your Doodle for a *lifetime of confidence and adaptability.*

Next Up: Socialization & Sensory Sensitivity—Building a Confident, Well-Adjusted Doodle

Your puppy is learning to love their crate—but confidence isn't just about being alone. It's also about feeling comfortable in new environments, meeting new people, and handling everyday life with ease.

In the next chapter, we'll break down:

- How to socialize your Doodle the right way—without creating overstimulation or fear

- How to avoid common mistakes that can make socialization overwhelming

Turn the page to learn how to introduce your Doodle to the world in a way that builds confidence, not fear.

Chapter 10

Socialization and Sensory Sensitivity

A Step-by-Step Guide to Raising a Confident, Resilient Doodle

I f Your Doodle gets overwhelmed by the world—or seems to react to *everything*—you're not alone. This chapter will help you build calm from the inside out so your Doodle can thrive in any environment.

Is This Chapter for You?

Socialization is one of the *most misunderstood* parts of raising a *well-adjusted Doodle*.

Many puppy parents assume that socialization just means meeting new people and dogs.

But true socialization is much more than that—it's about exposing your Doodle to the world in a way that:

- Builds confidence

- Prevents overstimulation

- Teaches them how to navigate new environments calmly

If Your Doodle:

- Gets overwhelmed in new places or around new people?

- Barks at strangers, noises, or unfamiliar objects?

- Struggles with grooming, vet visits, or handling?

- Is overly excited, or nervous, in social settings?

... then this chapter will help you *structure socialization the right way.*

By integrating socialization into **The Doodle Daily Schedule Blueprint™**, you can help your puppy develop *resilience, confidence, and the ability to settle in any environment.*

Why Socialization Is More Than Just Exposure

Many well-meaning puppy parents keep their puppies inside until fully vaccinated—only to spend months (or years) trying to undo the resulting anxiety and reactivity.

My own dog, Hershey, came to me at 16 weeks old, and I spent years carefully introducing her to the world she had missed during that critical early window.

While she made incredible progress, I saw firsthand how much harder it is to build confidence later.

That's why the **American Veterinary Society of Animal Behavior (AVSAB)** strongly recommends *early socialization, even before a puppy is fully vaccinated.*

> *"Incomplete or improper socialization during this critical time period can increase the risk of behavioral problems later in life, including fear, avoidance, and aggression. Behavioral issues, not infectious diseases, are the number one cause of death for dogs under three years of age."*
> —AVSAB Position Statement on Puppy Socialization (2021)

This means that *waiting too long to socialize your puppy can have lifelong consequences.*

But socialization isn't about doing as much as possible—it's about making sure each experience is positive and manageable for your puppy.

Marge Rogers and Eileen Anderson, co-authors of *Puppy Socialization: What It Is and How to Do It*, explain that quality matters more than quantity:

- Well-structured socialization builds confidence.

- Overexposure can actually lead to fear and overstimulation.

- Socialization should be tailored to your Doodle's personality.

Want expert insights? Listen to my interview with Marge Rogers and Eileen Anderson **The Doodle Pro® Podcast**, where they share their *best strategies for setting puppies up for lifelong confidence.*

Listen now: Part one at thedoodlepro.com/22 & part 2 at thedoodlepro.com/23

> *"Positive early exposure shapes a puppy's worldview. When we get it right, we're not just raising a well-behaved dog—we're raising a secure and emotionally healthy one."*
> —Jane Messineo Lindquist, Creator of Puppy Culture

The Doodle Socialization Blueprint™: Structure & Scheduling

Instead of overwhelming your puppy with random experiences, socialization should follow a structured schedule that gradually introduces new environments, people, and handling in a way they can process. Integrating socialization into **The Doodle Daily Schedule Blueprint™** helps your puppy feel safe while learning new things.

The Ongoing Socialization Loop

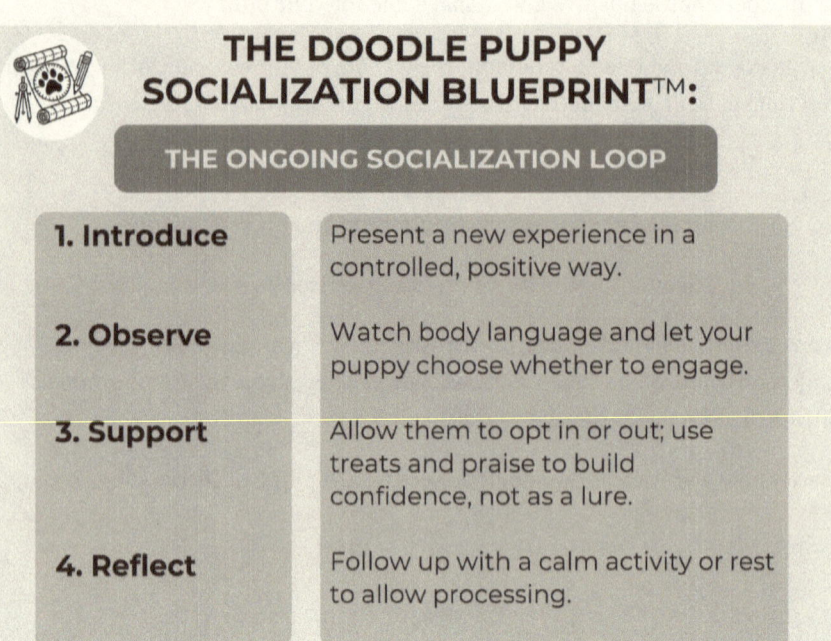

THE DOODLE PUPPY SOCIALIZATION BLUEPRINT™:

THE ONGOING SOCIALIZATION LOOP

1. Introduce	Present a new experience in a controlled, positive way.
2. Observe	Watch body language and let your puppy choose whether to engage.
3. Support	Allow them to opt in or out; use treats and praise to build confidence, not as a lure.
4. Reflect	Follow up with a calm activity or rest to allow processing.

Socialization isn't a one-time event—it's an ongoing process throughout your Doodle's life. That's why I developed The **Ongoing Socialization Loop** to ensure your puppy learns at their own pace in a positive way.

- **Introduce**: Present a new experience in a controlled, confidence-building way.

- **Observe**: Watch their body language to determine their comfort level.

- **Support**: Allow them to opt in or out, using treats and praise to build confidence.

- **Reflect**: Follow up with a calm activity or rest to let them process.

This loop builds resilience—helping your Doodle navigate new situations with ease.

Core Elements of Socialization

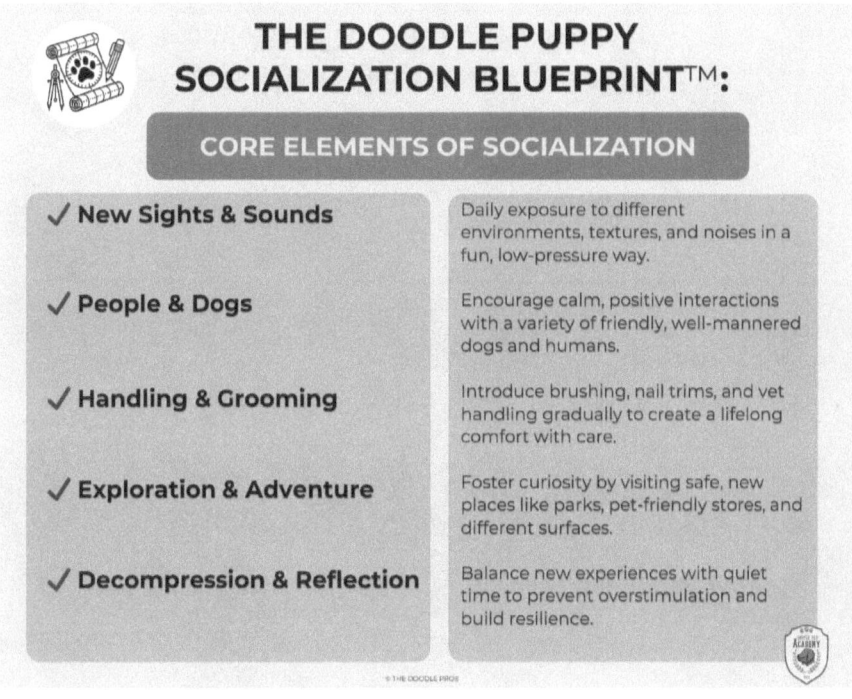

Socialization is more than meeting new dogs—it's about full sensory exposure in a structured way. The Core Elements of Socialization cover the key areas to focus on:

- **New Sights & Sounds** – Introduce different environments, textures, and noises gradually.

- **People & Dogs** – Encourage calm, positive interactions with friendly, well-mannered individuals.

- **Handling & Grooming** – Make vet visits and grooming stress-free by practicing at home.

- **Exploration & Adventure** – Visit new places (parks, pet-friendly stores) to foster curiosity.

- **Decompression & Reflection** – Balance social outings with rest to prevent overstimulation.

By thoughtfully exposing your Doodle to all these elements, you'll prevent future fear-based behaviors.

Key Principles of Socialization

THE DOODLE PUPPY SOCIALIZATION BLUEPRINT™:

KEY PRINCIPLES

✓ **Choice builds confidence**	Let your puppy decide whether to interact or explore at their own pace.
✓ **Socialization isn't just about meeting dogs**	It's about exposure to the full world in a way that fosters security.
✓ **Prioritize quality over quantity**	A few great interactions are better than many rushed or overwhelming ones.
✓ **Adapt to your puppy's personality**	Some may need slower introductions, while others thrive on variety.
✓ **Keep experiences short, positive, and stress-free**	This creates a well-adjusted, happy companion.

© THE DOODLE PRO®

The way you socialize your Doodle matters just as much as what they experience. Here are the Key Principles of Socialization to keep in mind:

- **Choice builds confidence** – Let your puppy decide whether to interact at their own pace.

- **It's not just about meeting dogs** – Socialization is about the full world, not just other pets.

- **Prioritize quality over quantity** – A few great interactions are better than overwhelming ones.

- **Adapt to your puppy's personality** – Some thrive on variety, while others need slow introductions.

- **Keep it short, positive, and stress-free** – Prevent overstimulation with manageable experiences.

When socialization is done correctly, it creates a well-adjusted, confident, and calm companion.

When Too Much Socialization Can Backfire

It's easy to assume that more exposure means better results. But flooding your puppy with new experiences—especially without proper recovery time—can do more harm than good.

- Puppies who experience too much, too fast—without structure—may develop demand barking and reactivity.

- Too much exposure can lead to reactivity, as their nervous system struggles to process too much, too fast.

- Dogs need decompression time to mentally process new experiences and prevent stress build-up.

The Doodle Daily Schedule Blueprint™ ensures that socialization is balanced with predictable rest periods, reducing the risk of overstimulation and reactivity.

Using the Doodle Pro Socialization Checklist

The Doodle Socialization Checklist is designed to help you track the experiences your puppy has—and the ones they haven't yet encountered. It serves as a guide to ensure your Doodle is thoughtfully introduced to a wide range of sights, sounds, and situations during their critical learning period.

Many families use this checklist as a fun scavenger hunt, making socialization something to look forward to. By using this tool, you can help buffer your puppy against future anxiety by pairing new experiences with positive, happy exposures during their most impressionable stage.

 **Download your printable checklist in the Doodle Daily Toolkit™ at : thedoodlepro.com/bonustoolkit**

Next Up: Managing Overstimulation & Stress

Socialization is essential—but too much, too fast, can backfire. If your Doodle gets overwhelmed, jumps on guests, or can't settle after outings, they may be struggling with sensory overload.

In the next chapter, we'll teach you:

- How to recognize the early signs of overstimulation

- How to help your Doodle find calm in any situation

- The best ways to balance engagement with proper rest

Turn the page to learn how to manage overstimulation and stress so your Doodle can stay confident and balanced.

Part 4

Managing Doodle Behavior & Common Challenges

"Doodles don't just grow out of bad habits. They grow into the routines we reinforce daily."

— The Doodle Pro®

Chapter 11

Overstimulation and Stress

A Step-by-Step Guide to Helping Your Doodle Regulate Their Emotions and Recover from Sensory Overload

I f your Doodle seems stuck in overdrive—wired, wild, or worried—this chapter will help you press the reset button.

Even with *thoughtful socialization*, some Doodles struggle with *sensory overload*.

If Your Doodle:

- Gets overexcited in new environments and can't settle?

- Barks, jumps, or lunges when overstimulated?

- Struggles with handling, grooming, or loud noises?

- Seems to be on edge instead of enjoying outings?

... then this chapter will help you recognize the signs of overstimulation and adjust their daily schedule. The goal? Calm confidence built through predictability.

The **Doodle Daily Schedule Blueprint™** ensures that mental recovery is just as important as activity, incorporating structured decompression time throughout the day.

Why Some Doodles Are Extra Sensitive to the World Around Them

Doodles are *intelligent, social, and highly aware* of their surroundings—which can make them *prone to sensory overload.*

Why Certain Breed Traits Make Doodles More Sensitive

- **Poodles:** Highly intelligent and responsive—quick to notice subtle changes.

- **Retrievers/Herders:** Thrive on interaction; can become frustrated when it's unpredictable.

- **Guardian breeds (e.g., Bernese Mountain Dogs):** May hesitate before engaging—and need space to assess.

- **Sporting breeds:** Bred for bursts of energy—prone to jumping or spinning without guidance.

Many Doodles experience *conflicted feelings* in social situations, especially when *meeting new people.*
Jumping may look like excitement, but for many dogs, it's a coping strategy—a way to create distance when they feel overwhelmed. Just like some dogs use licking as a *kiss-off instead of affection,* jumping can be a way to *gain distance when a dog feels overstimulated or unsure.*

Without *structured decompression time,* Doodles can become overstimulated, leading to:

- Barking, jumping, reactivity, or difficulty settling

- Sensory overload from too many experiences without rest

- Increased stress levels that can lead to long-term anxiety

Key Takeaway

Some Doodles struggle not because they need more exposure, but because they need time to process those experiences without pressure—which is exactly why **The Doodle Daily Schedule Blueprint™** incorporates decompression periods throughout the day.

Why "They Just Need to Get Used to It" Is a Myth

Many people believe that a dog who is fearful or overstimulated just needs more exposure until they "get used to it."

But research shows that *flooding a dog with stimulation before they're ready can actually increase fear rather than reduce it.*

- Dogs don't just "get over" fear—they need structure and choice to build confidence.

- Habituation happens when exposure is gradual, predictable, and allows the dog to disengage *(McMillan, 2017).*

- Left alone, *fear grows.* Behavior expert Suzanne Clothier emphasizes that fear doesn't resolve on its own—it compounds when a dog is repeatedly exposed to overwhelming situations.

- Overexposure can lead to learned helplessness. If a dog is repeatedly put in overwhelming situations without control or escape, they may stop reacting externally—but their stress levels remain high *(Seligman, 1967).*

In my discussion with **Dr. Zazie Todd**, author of *Bark*, we talked about the common myth that dogs *"just need to get used to"* things that scare them. She explained:

> *"Everybody has something that they're afraid of that perhaps is not entirely rational. It helps us empathize with our dogs because we can think, 'This isn't just our dogs being stupid. Actually, we know something about what that feels like.' So we can see it more from our dog's point of view, and I think that's helpful in helping our dogs to feel safe and safe with us."*
>
> —Dr. Zazie Todd, The Doodle Pro® Podcast

By understanding that *fear doesn't simply go away with more exposure,* we can approach our Doodle's training with *more patience, compassion, and structure,* ensuring that they feel *safe and supported.*

Flooding a dog with overwhelming experiences doesn't help them adjust—it can actually make their fear worse. Instead, gradual and positive exposure, where the dog feels safe and has choices, is key to building confidence. Listen to my full conversation with **Dr. Zazie Todd at thedoodlepro.com/67.**

Key Takeaway

More exposure isn't always better. For fearful or overstimulated Doodles, controlled exposure with choice and safety builds true confidence.

Case Study: How Luna Learned to Stay Calm When Guests Arrived
Cockapoo Luna's Struggle

- Loved people—but couldn't contain herself when guests arrived

- Would bark, spin in circles, and jump all over visitors the second they walked in

- If not allowed to greet, she would whine, pace, and paw at the door

Her family thought she was just excited—but her behaviors *weren't a sign of joy.*
They were a sign of *stress and overstimulation.*

The Changes That Helped Luna

- **Before guests arrived:** Luna had a short sniffari walk or a food puzzle to engage her brain and lower her arousal.

- **During visits:** Instead of rushing to greet visitors, she stayed on a mat with a chew toy, learning to relax while guests settled in.

- **Next step:** Once she could remain calm, they used *Go Say Hi* from my **Zoomies to Zen™** course to teach her how to *greet politely without jumping.*

Within a few weeks, Luna no longer charged the door. She had learned that guests were no longer overwhelming—just another part of her routine.

The Doodle Decompression Schedule: Preventing Overload

If your Doodle frequently struggles with *overstimulation,* adding *structured decompression time* to their daily routine can prevent *stress buildup.*

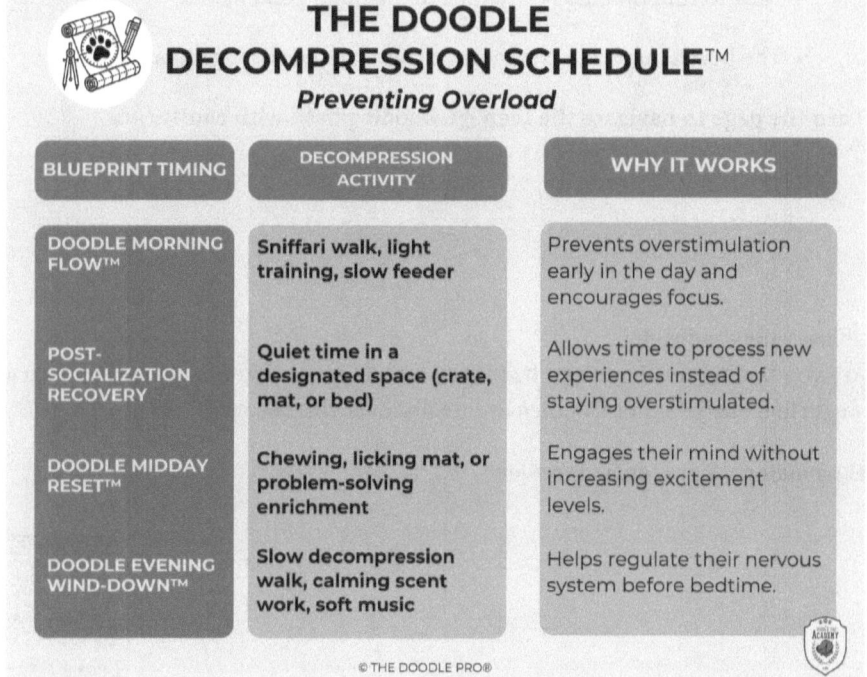

Key Takeaway

Overstimulation is often caused by too much excitement without enough processing time. Adding structured decompression to their Blueprint-based schedule prevents stress buildup before it turns into reactivity or avoidance.

Next Up: The Adolescent Doodle: Navigating the Teenage Phase

You've worked hard to create structure and manage energy levels—but then, *adolescence hits.*

Suddenly, your once *well-mannered Doodle* is ignoring commands, testing limits, and acting like they've forgotten everything you've taught them.

In the next chapter, we'll break down:

- Why adolescence isn't regression—it's a normal phase that requires structure

- How to reinforce daily rhythms to maintain good habits

- The best schedule adjustments to survive the teenage phase

Turn the page to navigate the teenage Doodle phase with confidence.

Share Your Feedback
Are you finding this Blueprint helpful so far? A quick review on Amazon—even a single line—helps other Doodle parents discover this resource.

thedoodlepro.com/amazonreview

Leave a review on Amazon.

Chapter 12

The Adolescent Doodle Schedule

Surviving the Teenage Phase

How to Prevent Training Regression, Manage Impulse Control, and Keep Your Sanity

If your Doodle suddenly forgot everything they ever learned—welcome to the teenage phase. This chapter will help you survive it, with your sanity (and socks) intact.

What Happened to My Sweet, Well-Behaved Puppy?

One day, your Doodle is following cues like a pro.

The next? They're jumping on guests, dragging you down the sidewalk, and stealing food off the counter like they've never heard the word "*leave it*" in their life.

Your calm, predictable puppy has been replaced by a wild, rebellious teenager—and it's exhausting.

Many Doodle parents assume that once puppyhood is over, the hard part's done. But *adolescence brings a whole new set of challenges*, as Rahul and Simran learned with their Poochon, Nala.

> **Nala's Adolescent Phase—A Story Every Doodle Parent Can Relate To**
>
> Rahul and Simran couldn't believe how well-behaved Nala was as a puppy. She learned **sit**, stayed **calm in the house**, and never chewed things she wasn't supposed to.
>
> *"Then one day, she just... stopped listening,"* Simran said. *"It was like she forgot all of her training overnight."*
>
> At nine months old, Nala was officially an adolescent. Instead of staying calm, she started testing every boundary—barking for attention, stealing socks, and conveniently "forgetting" commands she had mastered months ago.
>
> Instead of panicking or assuming she was a bad dog, Rahul and Simran stuck to **The Adolescent Doodle Schedule™**, reinforcing calm behavior with structured engagement.
>
> *"It wasn't easy,"* Rahul admitted. *"But once we stopped trying to 'fix' her and started reinforcing her daily rhythm, things smoothed out again."*
>
> **Key Takeaway**
> **Adolescence is not regression—it's a normal phase that requires structure and patience.**

Why Training Regression Happens in Adolescence

If your Doodle's behavior suddenly feels like it's unraveling, you're not alone.

This isn't disobedience—it's adolescence. And it's temporary.

Common Adolescent Behaviors:

- **Ignoring cues they previously knew** ("Sit? What's that?")

- **Increased demand barking and frustration behaviors**

- **Jumping, mouthing, or testing boundaries more often**

- **More difficulty settling, even with a structured schedule**

This isn't backsliding—it's a healthy (if frustrating) part of canine development.

The Science Behind Adolescent Behavior

Doodles go through *two major developmental periods:*

1.   **The Puppy Learning Phase (8 weeks - 6 months)** – When they absorb information quickly and form early habits.

2.   **The Adolescent Testing Phase (6-18 months, sometimes up to 3 years!)** – When they start testing limits, just like human teenagers.

Why Does It Feel Like They've Forgotten Everything?

·   **Brain development is still in progress** – The prefrontal cortex (responsible for impulse control) is still maturing (*Horowitz*, 2016).

·   **They're more easily distracted** – The world suddenly seems more exciting, so previous training takes a back seat.

·   **Hormonal changes affect behavior** – Even with spay/neuter, adolescent hormone shifts still impact impulse control, energy, and social behavior.

The Adolescent Doodle Daily Schedule: Balancing Energy, Structure, and Rest

What Adolescent Doodles Need:

·   **The Doodle Morning Flow™** - To start the day with calm, not chaos

·   **The Doodle Midday Reset™** - To prevent afternoon overstimulation

·   **The Doodle Evening Wind-Down™** - To teach impulse control before bed

·   **Activity Balance** - Avoid "over-exercise = burnout" traps

The Adolescent Doodle Daily Schedule (Blueprint-Aligned)

Morning Reset (6:00 AM – 12:00 PM)

Begin the morning with structure, gradually increasing activity.

Start with a calm potty break and light training, followed by structured exuberant play to release energy in a productive way. Avoid chaotic, unstructured play that ramps up energy too quickly.

This period sets the tone for a calm, structured day by balancing movement, engagement, and rest.

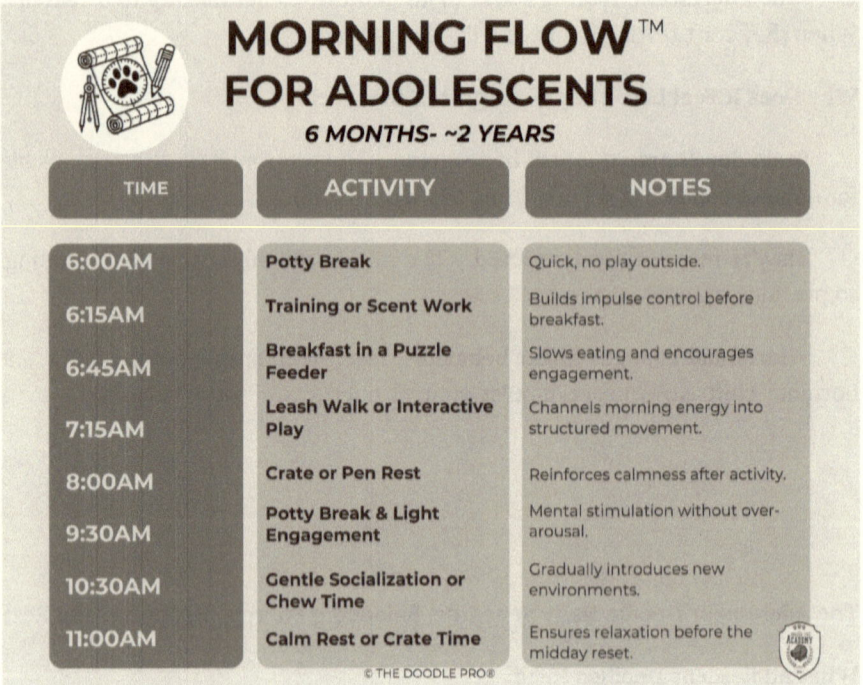

MORNING FLOW™ FOR ADOLESCENTS
6 MONTHS- ~2 YEARS

TIME	ACTIVITY	NOTES
6:00AM	Potty Break	Quick, no play outside.
6:15AM	Training or Scent Work	Builds impulse control before breakfast.
6:45AM	Breakfast in a Puzzle Feeder	Slows eating and encourages engagement.
7:15AM	Leash Walk or Interactive Play	Channels morning energy into structured movement.
8:00AM	Crate or Pen Rest	Reinforces calmness after activity.
9:30AM	Potty Break & Light Engagement	Mental stimulation without over-arousal.
10:30AM	Gentle Socialization or Chew Time	Gradually introduces new environments.
11:00AM	Calm Rest or Crate Time	Ensures relaxation before the midday reset.

© THE DOODLE PRO®

Grab your full-color printable version inside your Doodle Daily Toolkit™.

Midday Reset (12:00 PM – 3:00 PM)

If you are coming home for lunch or hiring a dog walker, adjust the routine accordingly:

· **If hiring a dog walker:** A structured leash walk can replace midday training or scent work, but keep it calm—no intense play or fetch.

· **If coming home for lunch:** Prioritize a calm potty break first—no high-energy play.

· Provide *mental enrichment* like a snuffle mat, frozen Kong, or a quick training refresher.

·   Reinforce *settling behaviors* before you or the walker leave again, using a chew toy or place training.

This period focuses on structured engagement, meals, and rest to set up a smooth afternoon.

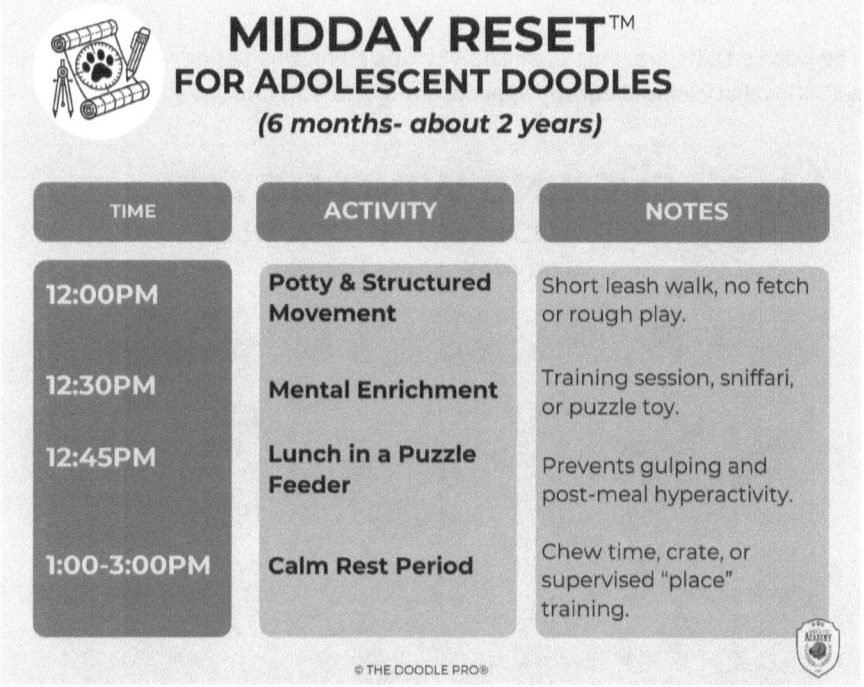

MIDDAY RESET™
FOR ADOLESCENT DOODLES
(6 months- about 2 years)

TIME	ACTIVITY	NOTES
12:00PM	Potty & Structured Movement	Short leash walk, no fetch or rough play.
12:30PM	Mental Enrichment	Training session, sniffari, or puzzle toy.
12:45PM	Lunch in a Puzzle Feeder	Prevents gulping and post-meal hyperactivity.
1:00-3:00PM	Calm Rest Period	Chew time, crate, or supervised "place" training.

© THE DOODLE PRO®

Evening Wind-Down (3:00 PM - 9:00 PM)

Evening play should be structured and timed appropriately to prevent overstimulation before bedtime.

High-energy activities like fetch or tug are best done earlier in the evening, followed by calming exercises such as a leash walk, puzzle toy, or light training to help transition into relaxation.

When Roughhousing Is Actually Helpful:
Roughhousing can be a great way to burn energy and strengthen your bond, but it needs *clear boundaries* (e.g., stopping on cue, no jumping or mouthing humans). It should only be included in designated high-energy play windows, such as *the morning (7:00 a.m. - 7:30 a.m.) or the Witching Hour (3:30 p.m. - 5:00 p.m.).*

This time of day is when puppies are most likely to experience:

· Zoomies

· Nipping

· Frustration behaviors

The *Doodle Daily Schedule Blueprint™* helps guide this period with structured activities that **channel energy appropriately** and lead into a restful night.

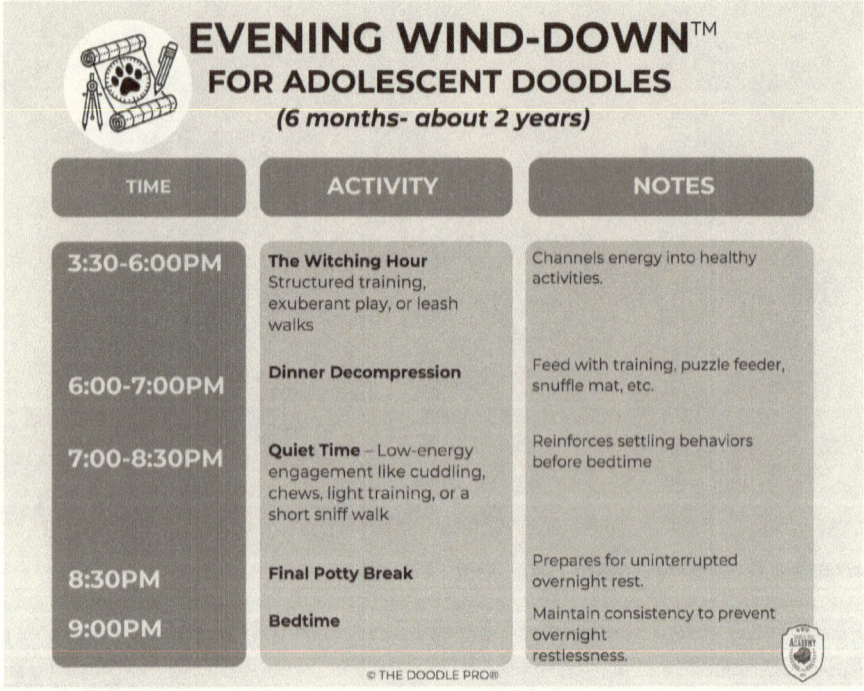

EVENING WIND-DOWN™
FOR ADOLESCENT DOODLES
(6 months- about 2 years)

TIME	ACTIVITY	NOTES
3:30-6:00PM	**The Witching Hour** Structured training, exuberant play, or leash walks	Channels energy into healthy activities.
6:00-7:00PM	**Dinner Decompression**	Feed with training, puzzle feeder, snuffle mat, etc.
7:00-8:30PM	**Quiet Time** – Low-energy engagement like cuddling, chews, light training, or a short sniff walk	Reinforces settling behaviors before bedtime
8:30PM	**Final Potty Break**	Prepares for uninterrupted overnight rest.
9:00PM	**Bedtime**	Maintain consistency to prevent overnight restlessness.

© THE DOODLE PRO®

The Science Behind Why Structure Works (And Why "Just Tire Them Out" Doesn't)

Let me share *three discoveries* from my **Doodle-boarding "lab" at Shed-FreeStay™** that completely changed how I approach teenage Doodles.

These aren't just theories—they're backed by research that explains exactly why some approaches work better than others during this challenging phase.

1. The Power of Predictability: Why Clear Routines Create Calm

·   Dr. Hiby's research (2006) found that dogs without predictable schedules experience higher cortisol (stress hormone) levels.

·   Instead of relaxing between activities, their *brains stay on high alert*—constantly wondering, "*What's next?*"

·   One client's adolescent Bernedoodle **transformed from chaos to calm** once we established *clear daily patterns*.

"*It's like he finally believes good things will happen without him having to make them happen,*" his parent told me.

2. The Balance of Activity & Recovery: Why "Tiring Them Out" Backfires

·   Research on working dogs (Blackwell et al., 2013) shows that excessive exercise builds endurance, not calmness.

·   One client's nine-month-old Goldendoodle was running five miles a day but still couldn't settle.

·   Instead of more physical exercise, we introduced mental stimulation, problem-solving tasks, and structured downtime.

·   Within weeks, her Doodle went from pacing all evening to actually choosing to rest.

3. Decision Fatigue & Impulse Control: Why More Choices = More Stress

·   Dogs, like people, experience decision fatigue. The more they have to figure out their schedule, the harder impulse control becomes (*McGreevy et al., 2018*).

·   One client's seven-month-old Aussiedoodle couldn't settle because he was constantly seeking direction.

·   We removed uncertainty by giving him a structured daily schedule with clear transitions between activity and rest.

·   Within a week, he went from nonstop movement to actually lying down on his own.

 **Your printable Adolescent Doodle Schedules are ready inside your toolkit at thedoodlepro.com/bonustoolkit.**

Next Up: Housetraining Regression & Setbacks: How to Reset Your Routine

You've worked hard to reinforce good habits, but just when you think you're in the clear, *your Doodle starts having accidents again.*

Let's talk about *why this happens—and how to fix it fast.*

Turn the page to reset your potty routine and ditch the frustration (again).

Chapter 13

Potty Training Setbacks and Regression

Why Accidents Happen and How to Get Back on Track

I f your Doodle was doing great— and now you're back to cleaning up puddles— you're not failing. This chapter will help you understand what changed and how to fix it.

Is This Chapter for You?

If your Doodle was once fully house-trained but is suddenly having accidents again, changes in routine may be the cause.

Has your Doodle started having accidents after a schedule disruption, such as a new work routine, travel, or moving homes?

Does it seem like your adolescent Doodle has forgotten their potty training?

Is your dog struggling with potty reliability at specific times of the day?

If so, this chapter will help you identify the cause, adjust their schedule, and reinforce good habits to prevent future accidents.

The **Doodle Daily Schedule Blueprint™** ensures predictable potty habits. By reinforcing a structured rhythm, you'll create a routine that prevents regression and sets your Doodle up for long-term success.

Why Potty Training Regression Happens

Many puppy parents assume that once a dog is *house-trained, they are house-trained for life.*

However, dogs, like people, develop habits based on *consistency*—if something disrupts their routine, *accidents can return.*

Common Causes of Potty Training Setbacks

- **Changes in Routine** – A new work schedule, travel, or moving homes can throw off a Doodle's potty rhythm.

- **Adolescence and Testing Boundaries** – Between six and eighteen months, dogs naturally go through a developmental phase where they may temporarily forget established habits.

- **Too Much Freedom Too Soon** – If a Doodle suddenly gains more access to the house without regular potty breaks, accidents can return.

- **Inconsistent Supervision** – If a puppy or adolescent dog is left unattended for too long between breaks, they may have accidents simply because they weren't given an opportunity to go outside.

Scent Matters: Why Old Smells Can Trigger Accidents

Even if your Doodle has been *house-trained for months, old pet odors can cause confusion*—especially in a new environment.

When we moved into a new home, my adolescent pup, Hershey, who had been completely house-trained, suddenly started having accidents in the basement.

At first, I was confused. Then I discovered—with a blacklight, no less—that the previous tenants' dogs had occasional accidents there.

Even though I hadn't noticed the smell, Hershey could.

Ew.

I was grossed out to realize those stains had been there all along, and I immediately rented a carpet cleaner. I also restricted Hershey's access to the basement while reinforcing her regular potty routine to prevent a habit from forming.

A similar issue happens in pet-friendly hotels. A well-trained male dog who never marks indoors may suddenly start lifting his leg when he detects invisible markings from other visiting dogs.

To him, the scent signals that marking is acceptable—even if it has never been a habit at home.

How to Prevent Scent-Based Accidents

A *two-step approach* is the best way to *prevent scent-triggered accidents*:

1. Use an enzymatic pet cleaner to break down old urine odors. Regular household cleaners may remove the smell for us, but dogs can still detect it.

2. Return to structured potty breaks with on-leash supervision until the habit is reinforced again.

The **Doodle Daily Schedule Blueprint™** incorporates *predictable potty breaks throughout the day* to prevent *scent-triggered accidents*.

How to Adjust Your Doodle's Schedule to Fix Potty Setbacks

Reinforcing a structured schedule is the best way to reset your Doodle's potty habits.

1. Reinforce the "Eat, Play, Sleep = Potty" Rule

A simple way to predict when your Doodle will need to go is to take them out after three key events:

- **After Eating** – Digestion triggers the need to eliminate, usually within five to thirty minutes.

- **After Playing** – Physical activity stimulates the bladder and bowels.

- **After Sleeping** – Puppies wake up and need to go immediately—do not wait.

Keeping *potty breaks predictable prevents accidents*.

The **Doodle Daily Schedule Blueprint™** ensures that potty breaks happen at the right moments, reinforcing a structured rhythm that makes house training stick.

 **Track your progress with the printable potty schedule included in The Doodle Daily Toolkit™.**

Download your copy: thedoodlepro.com/bonustoolkit

2. Adjust Timing Based on Life Changes

If your *schedule has changed*, your Doodle's schedule needs to *change with it*.

- **A new work schedule?** Shift potty breaks *gradually* so they align with your *updated availability*.

- **Recently traveled?** Expect *temporary setbacks* and schedule *more frequent breaks*.

- **More freedom in the house?** *Supervise closely* and *reduce access temporarily* if accidents return.

Most *potty regression resolves quickly* when the *schedule is adjusted and reinforced*.

3. Strengthen Potty Break Cues

If accidents happen because your Doodle is not signaling when they need to go, make sure they have a clear way to communicate:

- Stick to a structured schedule so they learn when potty time happens.

- Take them out on-leash to reinforce that potty breaks are for business, not playtime.

- Use a consistent phrase such as "Go potty" so they associate the cue with the action.

If your dog is struggling to signal, bell training can be an effective way for them to alert you when they need to go out.

The **Doodle Daily Schedule Blueprint™** reinforces routine potty cues, reducing accidents over time.

The Science Behind Why Schedules Prevent Accidents

- Dr. Hiby's research (2006) found that dogs with structured routines have lower cortisol (stress hormone) levels and exhibit calmer behavior.

- Arhant et al. (2010) found that accidents create a new habit—if a dog eliminates inside and is not interrupted, they may begin associating that surface with potty time.

- Dr. Overall's research (2013) emphasized that timing matters—puppies and adolescent dogs have limited bladder control, and skipping a scheduled break increases the chance of an accident.

The **Doodle Daily Schedule Blueprint™** makes *potty training part of a seamless daily rhythm.*

Stick with the rhythm. Stay consistent. Accidents become rare—even with a rebellious teenager.

Next Up: Managing Your Doodle's Daily Routine While Working from Home

Whether you're on back-to-back Teams meetings, a stay-at-home parent juggling tasks, or navigating a hybrid work schedule, keeping your Doodle's routine on track can feel like a challenge.

In the next chapter, we'll troubleshoot:

- How to set up a predictable routine that keeps your Doodle engaged without over-dependence on you.

- How to prevent demand barking, restlessness, and midday chaos.

- How to make hybrid schedules work—so your Doodle thrives whether you're home or away.

Turn the page to build a structure that supports your workflow—and your Doodle's needs.

Chapter 14

Work From Home Life With a Doodle

Creating Structure So You Can Focus While Your Doodle Thrives

I f your Doodle thinks *you being home* means it's playtime all day, this chapter will help you reclaim your schedule— without sacrificing your bond.

Is This Chapter for You?

Working from home with a Doodle sounds like a dream—until reality hits. Whether you work remotely full-time, split your days between home and the office, or manage the chaos of being a stay-at-home parent, one thing is clear: your Doodle doesn't automatically understand work hours.

Does Your Doodle:

- Bark, pace, or demand attention while you work?

- Turn Zoom meetings into a battle to keep them quiet?

- Struggle to understand when it's time to engage versus when to settle?

- Interrupt you like a furry toddler every time you sit down?

This chapter will guide you in creating a structured routine that keeps your Doodle engaged, prevents interruptions, and allows both of you to focus. A predictable daily schedule is the key to balance. The **Doodle Daily Schedule Blueprint™** helps structure your workday so that your Doodle learns when to expect engagement and when to settle independently.

 **Toolkit Reminder:**

Find a customizable **Work-From-Home Routine Template** in **The Doodle Daily Toolkit™. Download your copy:** thedoodlepro.com/bonustoolkit

The Most Common Work-from-Home Struggles

Many Doodle parents quickly realize that being home all day doesn't guarantee a well-behaved dog. Without structure, frustration builds on both ends.

1. Demand Barking & Attention-Seeking

Doodles are social, intelligent dogs. If they bark and receive any response—even a "shhh" or a tossed toy—they learn that barking works.

Why It Happens:

Doodles don't instinctively know when it's "work mode" versus "playtime."

They only know that their human is home and available.

The Fix:

- Set predictable engagement times so they learn when to expect interaction.

- Reinforce settle cues using place training or a relaxation mat.

- Use a frozen Kong, snuffle mat, or chew toy for independent entertainment during focus hours.

2. The Endless Door Game

Does working from home make you feel like a full-time doorman? You just sat down when your Doodle starts pawing at the door. Maybe this time it's urgent?

But no—they step outside, sniff the air, stare at a leaf, then request reentry like a VIP at a nightclub.

Why It Happens:

Doodles invent reasons to interrupt because interruptions get your attention.

The Fix:

- Create a structured potty schedule within **The Doodle Daily Schedule Blueprint™** so they learn when to expect outside time.

- Teach a "Settle Spot" (a mat or crate) near your workspace for quiet time.

- Ignore non-urgent door requests—reward patience, not persistence.

3. Zoomies & Mischief During Meetings

Right before an important call? That's when the zoomies hit. Bored Doodles invent their own entertainment—counter-surfing, shredding papers, or, in Maisie's case, parading through the background of every virtual meeting.

Case Study: Maisie the Zoom Star

Maisie, a three-year-old Labradoodle, had a knack for making surprise guest appearances in Zoom meetings. Her mom, Danielle, had tried everything—closing the office door, setting up a cozy bed, even handing Maisie a frozen Kong. At first, her coworkers laughed it off—who doesn't love a goofy Doodle cameo? But after a few too many interruptions, her supervisor mentioned that the calls were starting to feel unprofessional. It wasn't until Danielle introduced a predictable daily rhythm that Maisie learned when to settle—and when it was time for play.

Adapting to a Hybrid Work Schedule

Hybrid work adds another challenge—your Doodle doesn't just need a work-from-home routine but also a plan for the days you leave the house.

How to Balance Office & Home Days:

- Keep meal and potty times consistent across both home and office days.

- On office days, use enrichment toys like a frozen Kong before leaving.

- Teach independent settling so your Doodle can relax even when you're home.

- Adjust engagement accordingly. If they get a long midday walk on office days, try mental enrichment at home to balance it out.

Stay-at-Home Parent Doodle Routine

Raising a Doodle while juggling kids is work. Managing a household means balancing a busy family schedule, but your Doodle still needs structure.

How to Balance Raising a Doodle While Parenting at Home

- Sync routines. If your child has a morning nap or quiet time, use that for your Doodle's crate time or independent play.

- Create kid-safe enrichment stations. A frozen Kong, snuffle mat, or "Doodle toy bin" near the playroom can keep your pup engaged. This is excellent for "trading" your Doodle's toys when they inevitably go to chew on a child's toy.

- Teach a 'Settle Spot.' Use a designated mat or bed where your Doodle can relax while you cook dinner or do schoolwork with older kids.

- Avoid overstimulation. If your child and Doodle both get hyper together, redirect them into structured activities.

Sample Work-from-Home & Hybrid Schedule

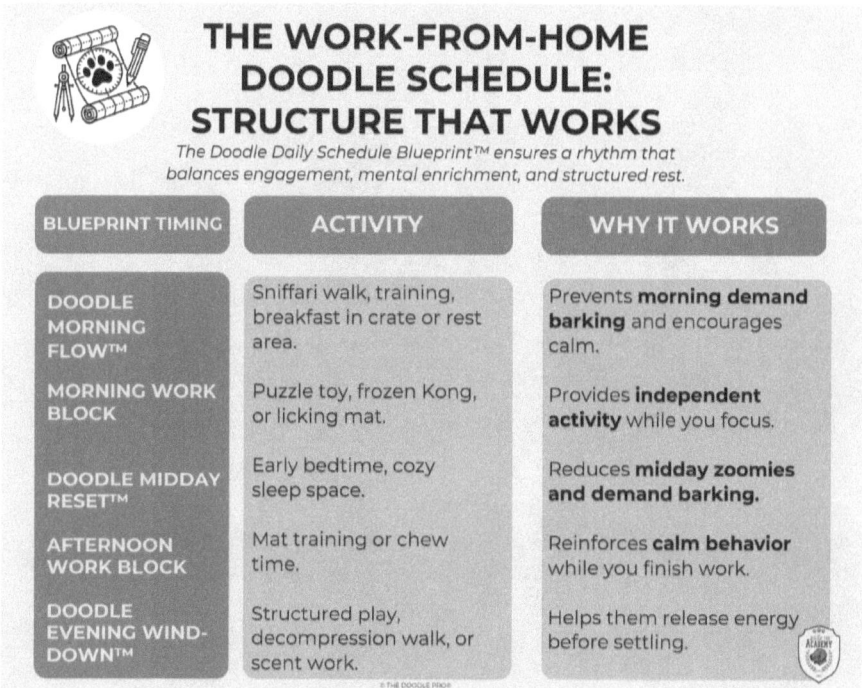

THE WORK-FROM-HOME DOODLE SCHEDULE: STRUCTURE THAT WORKS

The Doodle Daily Schedule Blueprint™ ensures a rhythm that balances engagement, mental enrichment, and structured rest.

BLUEPRINT TIMING	ACTIVITY	WHY IT WORKS
DOODLE MORNING FLOW™	Sniffari walk, training, breakfast in crate or rest area.	Prevents **morning demand barking** and encourages calm.
MORNING WORK BLOCK	Puzzle toy, frozen Kong, or licking mat.	Provides **independent activity** while you focus.
DOODLE MIDDAY RESET™	Early bedtime, cozy sleep space.	Reduces **midday zoomies and demand barking.**
AFTERNOON WORK BLOCK	Mat training or chew time.	Reinforces **calm behavior** while you finish work.
DOODLE EVENING WIND-DOWN™	Structured play, decompression walk, or scent work.	Helps them release energy before settling.

© THE DOODLE PRO®

Print your copy from the Toolkit, stick it by your desk, and stay one step ahead of the Doodle chaos.

Next Up: Keeping Structure Through Life's Transitions

Your Doodle is thriving on a structured routine—but what happens when life changes? New job, travel, kids going back to school—these transitions can disrupt even the best schedules. In the next chapter, we'll talk about how to keep things predictable, even when life is anything but.

Turn the page to stay structured—even when life gets unpredictable.

Part 5

Your Doodle's Well-Being & Adapting to Life's Changes

"Your Doodle's schedule won't stay the same forever—so their routine needs to evolve, too."

— The Doodle Pro®

Chapter 15

Customizing Your Doodle's Schedule for Your Lifestyle

How to Adjust Routines for Seasonal Changes, School Breaks, Life Transitions, and Recovery Periods

I f your "perfect schedule" keeps falling apart every time life changes, this chapter will show you how to pivot—without losing progress or your sanity.

Why Your Doodle's Schedule Should Evolve

Doodles thrive on *structure and predictability*, but life doesn't always cooperate.

- The schedule that works during the school year might not fit summer vacation.

- A routine that works for a high-energy adolescent might need adjusting as your Doodle matures.

- A plan that works when you're feeling great might fall apart if you're sick or recovering from surgery.

Instead of forcing *a rigid routine year-round*, the key is learning how to adapt your Doodle's schedule while maintaining structure. This doesn't mean abandoning routine—it means keeping the *predictability* while letting the *details* flex with your lifestyle.

Whether you work swing shifts, rotate between hybrid days, or chase soccer games on the weekends, your Doodle can still find calm through *anchor points*. These mini-patterns help your dog know what to expect—even if your schedule looks different every day.

Friendly Reminder: You can absolutely throw the schedule out the window for a day-long adventure or spontaneous fun; that's the beauty of this Blueprint. It's your rhythm to return to—not a rulebook you're bound to. This schedule is your home base, not your leash—it gives you a steady rhythm to return to, even after a chaotic or unexpected day.

The Blueprint ensures that no matter what changes happen, your Doodle's *core needs*—predictable feeding, exercise, rest, and enrichment—are still met, no matter what life throws at you.

How to Adapt the Schedule for Seasons & Weather

The seasons impact your Doodle's routine more than you might realize.

Changes in daylight, temperature, and human activity levels all affect your dog's behavior.

Summer vs. Winter Routines

- Longer daylight hours in summer often lead to more evening energy.

- Colder weather in winter may reduce outdoor exercise time.

- Changes in human schedules, such as vacations and holidays, can shift daily rhythms.

How to Adjust

- In hot weather, move walks to early morning or after sunset to avoid overheating. Use indoor enrichment, such as puzzle toys or snuffle mats, to replace physical exercise.

- In cold weather, shorten outdoor walks but increase mental stimulation. If it's too cold for long outings, structured indoor playtime helps maintain engagement.

Research on canine thermoregulation found that dogs naturally adjust their activity levels based on temperature, humidity, and daylight exposure (*King et al.*, 2019).

While your Doodle will adapt to seasonal shifts, structured schedule adjustments will help them transition more smoothly.

The **Doodle Daily Schedule Blueprint™** builds in flexibility for seasonal changes, keeping a consistent rhythm while adjusting exercise and enrichment activities to match the weather.

Preventing Routine Meltdowns During School Transitions

When kids are home from school, a Doodle's routine is often the *first thing to fall apart*.

How School Schedules Affect Your Doodle

- During the school year, the house is quiet for long stretches, then busy in the mornings and evenings.

- During school breaks and holidays, kids are home all day, routines shift, and the house's energy level increases significantly.

How to Keep a Doodle's Routine from Falling Apart During School Breaks

- Keep feeding, potty, and sleep schedules the same. Core routines (like feeding and sleep) are anchor points that keep your Doodle grounded—no matter how chaotic the rest of the day feels.

- Set expectations for kid-Doodle interactions. More excitement often leads to overstimulation. Having set quiet times for your Doodle prevents this.

- Plan Doodle-friendly family activities. If you're busy with the kids, include your Doodle in activities such as sniff walks, outdoor games, or quiet cuddle time.

- Prepare for the back-to-school transition early. If your Doodle has gotten used to constant company, practice short alone-time windows before the first day back—this prevents anxiety when the house suddenly empties out.

A 2022 study on household routine changes in dogs found that abrupt shifts in a dog's social environment and daily routine contribute to increased anxiety behaviors (*Hiby et al.*, 2022).

The **Doodle Daily Schedule Blueprint™** reinforces predictable structure, making back-to-school transitions smoother and reducing stress.

Case Study: Buddy the Whoodle Adjusts to Back-to-School Season
Doodle: Buddy, a two-year-old Whoodle
Situation: His routine changed drastically when his family's kids went back to school.
The Challenge

- He had constant attention all summer, but suddenly, the house was empty for hours.

- He started pacing, whining, and barking when left alone.

- By the end of the day, he was over-the-top excitable, jumping on the kids and grabbing at clothes when they got home.

What Was Missing?
Buddy wasn't just missing his family—he was struggling with the sudden loss of structure.
His family thought he was being extra needy, but in reality, he was experiencing schedule shock and didn't know how to settle himself. That's why consistent anchor points—even when life gets busy—an make all the difference in helping your Doodle feel grounded.
The Solution

- They started practicing alone time in short increments before school started.

- They kept feeding, potty, and bedtime schedules consistent, even if other activities shifted.

- They added a structured morning routine with a sniffari and short training session before the kids left to release mental energy.

- Instead of rough play when the kids got home, they gave Buddy a lick mat or frozen Kong while everyone settled in with snacks and homework.

Within two weeks, Buddy adjusted.
Instead of pacing and barking, he learned to settle during the day and greet the kids calmly in the afternoon. The Doodle Daily Schedule Blueprint™ ensured Buddy's routine was predictable and supportive, helping him transition smoothly.

When You're Not at 100%—Maintaining Structure with Minimal Effort

Even the *most* dedicated pet parents need a low-maintenance routine for days (or weeks) when they're not at full strength.

Your Doodle still needs structure, but you need to conserve energy.

How to Maintain Structure with Minimal Effort

- Stick to regular meal times—this is an easy way to maintain predictability.

- Don't skip engagement—just change the format. Use sniffing, puzzles, and calm tasks instead of long walks.

Even when you're not at your best, **The Doodle Daily Schedule Blueprint™** helps maintain structure, preventing behavioral regression.

Coming Soon: Raising the Perfect Doodle

Want expert insights on daycare, dog walkers, and advanced training strategies? In my next book, *Raising the Perfect Doodle: Training & Behavior Solutions*, I'll share insider knowledge from owning one of Denver's top dog-walking companies and nearly a decade of boarding and daycare for Doodles. Stay tuned!

Next Up: Preparing for Travel & Boarding

Routine disruptions *aren't just about schedule changes*—they also happen when you travel or board your Doodle.

Some Doodles adapt easily, while others struggle with separation anxiety or new environments.

In the next chapter, we'll show you how to keep your Doodle's routine intact while traveling—whether they're coming with you or staying behind.

Turn the page to learn how to make travel and boarding stress-free for both of you.

Chapter 16

Travel and Boarding Schedules

Keeping Routines Consistent, No Matter Where You Go

I f your Doodle turns into a bundle of stress the moment you pack a suitcase, this chapter will help you bring calm and consistency—wherever life takes you.

Is This Chapter for You?

Doodles thrive on *routine and predictability*, which is why travel, boarding, and schedule disruptions can be challenging.

Does Your Doodle:

- Struggle with new environments, like hotels, boarding facilities, or family homes?

- Get anxious when their routine changes?

- Have trouble settling when traveling or sleeping in a new place?

If so, this chapter will help you keep their schedule as consistent and stress-free as possible, even when you're on the go.

Why Travel and Boarding Disrupt Doodle Routines

Dogs rely on predictability to feel secure.

Changes in environment, routine, and caretakers can trigger stress responses in the brain, activating the hypothalamic-pituitary-adrenal (HPA) axis, which governs how dogs respond to unfamiliar situations (*McEwen & Wingfield, 2003*).

Through thousands of overnight stays with hundreds of Doodles, I tested and fine-tuned **The Doodle Daily Schedule Blueprint™** to see what actually works in real-world settings.

What I found was simple:

- Structure makes all the difference. The dogs who had predictable daily rhythms adjusted more smoothly.

- Familiar cues help Doodles settle faster. Consistent potty breaks, feeding times, and engagement periods helped even the most anxious dogs relax.

- Overexcitement can be just as stressful as anxiety. Too much stimulation—from new smells to non-stop play—can overwhelm the nervous system, leading to crankiness or trouble settling.

> **"The insights I gained from thousands of Doodles' overnight stays in my Doodle-exclusive training and boarding program helped me fine-tune *The Doodle Daily Schedule Blueprint™*, ensuring Doodles can thrive—wherever they are."**

Boarding Schedules: Setting Your Doodle Up for a Stress-Free Stay

If your Doodle will be staying at a boarding facility, sitter's home, or with family, here's how to make the transition smoother:

- Drop them off earlier in the day. This gives them time to explore, settle in, and adjust before their first night away.

- Keep drop-off calm and casual. If you linger or act anxious, your Doodle will pick up on your emotions. Keep it as routine as possible.

- Time your packing strategically. Many Doodles recognize suitcases as a sign of upcoming separation and may show stress before the trip even begins. Packing after they've been dropped off can prevent unnecessary anxiety.

A 2017 study on canine separation stress found that dogs exhibit higher vocalization and pacing behaviors in the first 24 hours of a new boarding environment but settle faster when familiar items (like blankets or toys) are provided (*Palestrini et al., 2017*).

The insights I gained from my boarding research shaped **The Doodle Daily Schedule Blueprint™** to create smoother transitions and stress-free adjustments.

After Boarding: Why Your Doodle May Seem "Sad" or "Mad"

Many parents expect their Doodle to greet them with over-the-top excitement after boarding.

But sometimes, the reaction is the opposite—quiet, withdrawn, or even seemingly "mad."

What's Actually Happening?

- Doodles need time to decompress. Even in a great facility or sitter's home, they've been adapting to new sights, smells, dogs, and routines. Their brain and body are tired. What they need the most is rest.

- High social interaction leads to exhaustion. If your Doodle has been around other dogs, they likely used a lot of mental energy navigating group dynamics.

Think of it like a toddler after an all-day birthday party—overtired, overstimulated, and needing rest.

Key Takeaway

This doesn't mean they didn't have fun. Even the most social dogs still need downtime after a long, exciting event with their favorite people.

A 2020 study on social fatigue in dogs found that dogs who engage in prolonged social interaction show increased signs of exhaustion and decreased responsiveness in the 24 hours following the experience (*Horváth et al., 2020*).

Through my work with boarding Doodles, I saw this pattern repeatedly—even in the most extroverted dogs.

The best thing you can do is give them space to rest and reset so they don't become overtired or cranky.

How to Help Your Doodle Reset After Boarding

- Let them sleep as much as they need—it's normal.

- Avoid over-exciting them with long play sessions or visitors right away.

- Give them space to settle before introducing new activities.

The strategies I tested at my boarding program became part of **The Doodle Daily Schedule Blueprint™,** ensuring that Doodles can smoothly transition between environments without unnecessary stress.

Next Up: Vet and Vaccination Schedules

Traveling can shake up a Doodle's routine—but so can another major event: vet visits.

Whether it's a routine checkup or a sudden health concern, many Doodles struggle with fear at the vet.

In the next chapter, we'll talk about:

- How to make vet visits easier.

- How to keep up with vaccinations.

- How to ensure your Doodle stays healthy for years to come.

Turn the page to create a proactive health routine your Doodle can count on—just like their daily schedule.

Chapter 17

Vet and Vaccination Schedule

How to Stay Organized, Reduce Vet Anxiety, and Keep Your Doodle's Care on Track

I f keeping up with vaccines, wellness checks, and vet visits feels overwhelming, this chapter will give you the structure (and tools) to make it manageable—for both you and your Doodle.

Keeping Your Doodle Healthy with Preventative Care

Is This Chapter for You?

- Not sure which vaccinations and vet visits your Doodle needs at each life stage?

- Want to prevent anxiety at the vet before it becomes an issue?

- Need an organized system to track appointments and health records?

Note: *This chapter is not intended to replace veterinary advice— always consult your vet for medical decisions specific to your Doodle.*

This chapter will help you stay on top of your Doodle's healthcare needs with a clear, age-based vet schedule—so you never miss an important vaccination, wellness check, or preventative care appointment.

Why a Vet and Vaccination Schedule Matters

A structured vet schedule does more than just keep appointments in order—it directly impacts your Doodle's longevity and quality of life.

- **Prevents serious illnesses** – Routine vet visits catch health issues early and ensure your Doodle is protected from preventable diseases.

- **Builds a positive association with the vet** – Regular, low-stress visits help prevent fear-based reactions later.

- **Keeps you organized** – Tracking vaccinations, checkups, and preventative care helps you stay ahead of health needs instead of reacting to problems.

A **2021 study on preventative veterinary care** found that **dogs with consistent wellness visits lived longer and had lower rates of emergency visits** (Wojciechowska et al., 2021).

Toolkit Reminder

Find the printable full-color version in your Doodle Daily Toolkit™.

thedoodlepro.com/bonustoolkit

The Importance of a Vet Visit After Gotcha Day

All new Doodles—whether puppies or adults—should see a *vet within the first few days of coming home.*

Why the First Vet Visit Matters:

- Ensures your new Doodle is healthy and up to date on vaccinations.

- Establishes a relationship with your vet early.

- Screens for parasites, underlying conditions, or past health issues that may not be obvious.

A 2019 study on newly adopted dogs found that early wellness exams reduced post-adoption health complications by 30% (*Patronek et al., 2019*).

Scheduling this first visit right away sets your Doodle up for a healthy transition into their new home.

Age-Based Vet & Vaccination Schedule

Doodles require different vet care at different life stages. Below is a general guideline for what to expect.

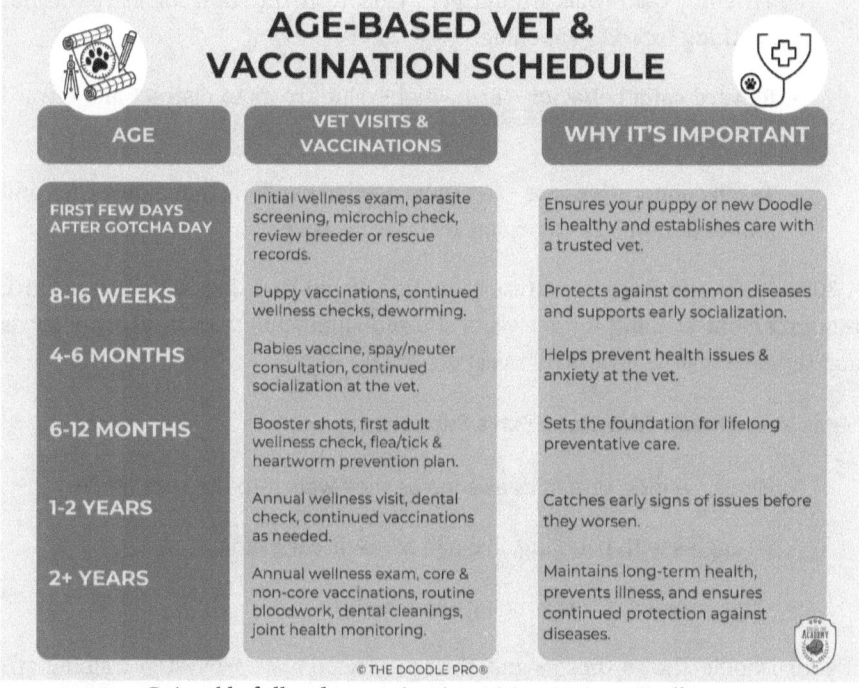

AGE	VET VISITS & VACCINATIONS	WHY IT'S IMPORTANT
FIRST FEW DAYS AFTER GOTCHA DAY	Initial wellness exam, parasite screening, microchip check, review breeder or rescue records.	Ensures your puppy or new Doodle is healthy and establishes care with a trusted vet.
8-16 WEEKS	Puppy vaccinations, continued wellness checks, deworming.	Protects against common diseases and supports early socialization.
4-6 MONTHS	Rabies vaccine, spay/neuter consultation, continued socialization at the vet.	Helps prevent health issues & anxiety at the vet.
6-12 MONTHS	Booster shots, first adult wellness check, flea/tick & heartworm prevention plan.	Sets the foundation for lifelong preventative care.
1-2 YEARS	Annual wellness visit, dental check, continued vaccinations as needed.	Catches early signs of issues before they worsen.
2+ YEARS	Annual wellness exam, core & non-core vaccinations, routine bloodwork, dental cleanings, joint health monitoring.	Maintains long-term health, prevents illness, and ensures continued protection against diseases.

© THE DOODLE PRO®

Printable full-color version is waiting in your Toolkit.

A 2020 study on vaccine efficacy found that core vaccinations in dogs provide strong immunity for up to three years, but annual wellness exams are still essential for early disease detection (Day et al., 2020).

Following this schedule ensures your Doodle stays healthy and comfortable with vet visits.

Helping Your Doodle Feel Comfortable at the Vet

Many Doodles develop anxiety about vet visits, especially if they only go when they're sick or in pain.

How to Prevent Vet Anxiety:

- **Practice positive exposure** -Take your Doodle to the vet's office just for a friendly visit—walk around, get a treat from the staff, and leave without anything "scary" happening.

- **Reward calm behavior** - Bring high-value treats to distract and reward them during exams.

- **Teach cooperative care** - Get them used to handling their paws, ears, and mouth at home so vet exams feel less invasive.

A 2022 study on veterinary stress reduction found that dogs who had positive reinforcement training for vet visits showed significantly lower cortisol levels and reduced fear behaviors (*Frank et al., 2022*).

Signs Your Doodle May Need Extra Support

- Paces, whines, or panics as soon as they walk into the vet's office.

- Struggles with handling, like nail trims or ear exams.

- Tries to avoid or resist being examined.

If your Doodle shows these signs, they may need a step-by-step training approach to become comfortable with vet visits.

That's why in my next book, *Raising the Perfect Doodle: Training & Behavior Solutions*, I cover how to train your Doodle to stay calm and cooperative at the vet—from desensitization exercises to handling practice at home.

Until then, catch my interview with cooperative care expert, Laura Monaco Torelli on collaborating with vets and groomers on the Doodle Pro® Podcast at thedoodlepro.com/47

Next Up: Grooming Maintenance & Doodle Coat Care

Vet care is just **one part of a healthy Doodle routine—grooming is just as essential**.

- How often should you trim nails, clean ears, and brush teeth?

- What's the best way to stay on top of coat maintenance and prevent matting?

- How do you create a low-stress grooming routine at home?

In the next chapter, we'll break down a Doodle-specific grooming schedule so you can stay ahead of maintenance and avoid common coat and skin issues.

Turn the page to build a grooming routine that prevents matting, reduces stress, and keeps your Doodle looking (and feeling) their best.

Chapter 18

Grooming Schedule

Keeping Up with Nails, Brushing, Teeth, Ear Care, and Coat Maintenance

How to Build a Realistic Grooming Routine That Works for You and Your Doodle—Without Mats, Mess, or Meltdowns

If grooming feels like a never-ending chore—or a constant source of guilt—you're not alone. This chapter will help you build a simple system that actually works.

Is This Chapter for You?

- Not sure how often to brush, bathe, or trim your Doodle's coat?

- Struggling with nail trims, ear cleaning, or tooth brushing?

- Want a grooming routine that keeps your Doodle comfortable and mat-free?

Note: This chapter provides practical guidance based on experience— not professional grooming certification. Always consult a trusted groomer or vet for concerns related to coat condition, allergies, skin issues, or specialized care.

This chapter will help you create a manageable, low-stress grooming schedule that fits your Doodle's needs and prevents common coat and health issues.

Why a Grooming Schedule Is Essential for Doodles

A *consistent grooming schedule* isn't just about *looks*—it's critical to your Doodle's *health and comfort.*

- **Prevents painful matting** - Doodles don't shed like other breeds, but their coat can quickly tangle and mat if not brushed regularly.

- **Keeps skin healthy** - Regular grooming removes debris, prevents irritation, and allows you to check for skin issues.

- **Reduces vet visits** - Nail trims, ear cleaning, and dental care help prevent infections, joint issues, and costly vet bills.

A 2021 study on canine coat maintenance found that dogs with routine brushing and grooming had lower rates of skin infections and reduced coat-related veterinary visits (*Miller et al., 2021*).

 **Toolkit Reminder**

Grab your printable Grooming Tracker anytime from **The Doodle Daily Toolkit™** at: **thedoodlepro.com/bonustoolkit**

Doodle Coats May Look Fine on the Surface, But...

Skipping regular brushing can lead to *painful matting.*

Tiana and Darius found this out *the hard way* with their Newfypoo, Biggie...

Tiana and Darius adored their giant, fluffy Newfypoo, Biggie—but one grooming mistake almost cost them his gorgeous coat.

"We brushed him sometimes, but his fur looked fine, so we figured we were good," Tiana said.

Then, the groomer found matting deep under his coat—so bad that Biggie had to be shaved down.

"We felt awful, we didn't even recognize him when we picked him up," Darius admitted. *"Now, we brush him every other day like we should've done from the start, AND check with a comb to make sure it's actually tangle-free!"*

Key Takeaway
Doodle coats may look fine on the surface, but skipping regular grooming leads to painful matting.

The Doodle Grooming Schedule: How to Stay Ahead of Mats and Mess

THE DOODLE GROOMING SCHEDULE
WHAT TO DO & WHEN

GROOMING TASK	FREQUENCY	WHY IT'S IMPORTANT
BRUSHING & COMBING	Daily or every other day	Prevents matting, reduces shedding, keeps coat clean.
NAIL TRIMMING	Every 2-4 weeks	Prevents overgrowth, joint strain, and painful cracks.
TEETH BRUSHING	Three to five times per week	Prevents tartar buildup, bad breath, and gum disease.
BATHING	Every four to six weeks or when dirty	Keeps coat fresh without stripping natural oils.
PROFESSIONAL GROOMING	Every four to six weeks (up to eight weeks for a very short sport cut)	Ensures coat is trimmed and manageable.

© THE DOODLE PRO®

A 2023 study on canine dermatology found that dogs bathed every four to six weeks with proper coat conditioning had healthier skin microbiomes than those bathed too frequently or too infrequently (*Rodriguez et al., 2023*).

Brushing: The Most Important Grooming Habit for Doodles

Brushing is *non-negotiable.*

Even short-coated Doodles need regular brushing to prevent painful mats.

How to Make Brushing Effective:

- **Use the right tools -** A slicker brush and metal comb work best for detangling.

- **Be thorough -** Focus on trouble spots like behind the ears, armpits, and under the collar.

- **Stay consistent -** Even five minutes a day prevents matting.

> "When we introduce brushing as a positive, predictable experience, dogs learn to participate willingly rather than resist. Cooperative care means working with your dog, not against them."
> —Laura Monaco Torelli, Certified Trainer & Husbandry Specialist

Matting isn't just an unsightly tangle—it can feel like walking around with duct tape pulling at their skin, especially under their armpits and around their neck.

Fear-Free Nail Trims: How to Make it Less Stressful for Everyone

My Doodle Pro® Honor Society members were shocked when my colleague, professional trainer and groomer Laura Stephens, shared some surprising insights with them about their Doodle's nails.

Keeping your Doodle's nails short means trimming them every 3-4 weeks. This sometimes means more often than when they get groomed. **Long nails, over time, will flatten the bones in your Doodle's feet, and put their wrists and spine in an unnatural position... permanently."**

—Laura Stephens, The Nerdy Nail Trimmer

Woah—that's more serious than just scratched hardwood, right?

Even now that you know how frequently they need it, your Doodle might not be convinced.

Many Doodles resist nail trims because they've had a bad experience or aren't used to handling.

How to Reduce Nail Trim Anxiety:

- **Start slow** – Introduce the nail clippers or grinder without trimming at first.

- **Reward micro-progress** - Celebrate small wins like touching paws, holding a foot, or tapping the nail clipper against a nail.

- **Use consent-based handling** - Let your Doodle opt-in to the process rather than restraining them.

"When we allow dogs to make choices in their grooming process—like voluntarily offering a paw for nail trims—it builds trust and reduces fear."

—Laura Monaco Torelli, The Doodle Pro® Podcast

A 2022 study on dog behavior and handling found that *dogs who were gradually desensitized to nail trims had significantly lower stress responses than those* restrained for forced trims *(Carter et al., 2022).*

Learn more from **Laura Monaco Torelli** about how to make grooming and veterinary care a positive experience for your Doodle on **The Doodle Pro® Podcast episodes #47 and #49.** *Plus, find a bonus guide on nail trimming from the* **Nerdy Nail Trimmer** *in your bonus* **Daily Doodle Toolkit™!**

Ear Cleaning: Preventing Infections in Floppy-Eared Doodles

- **Use a vet-approved ear cleaner** - Never use hydrogen peroxide or alcohol.

- **Check for redness or odor** - Early detection prevents bigger problems.

- **Wipe only what you can see** - Never insert anything deep into the ear canal.

If your Doodle hates ear cleaning, pair it with a high-value reward so they build a positive association.

Teeth Brushing: Avoiding Dental Disease Before It Starts

- **Start small** - Even a few swipes with pet-safe toothpaste is better than nothing.

- **Use a soft brush or finger brush** - Avoid human toothpaste, which is toxic to dogs.

- **Be consistent** - Aim for at least three times per week to prevent tartar buildup.

A 2021 study on canine dental health found that *dogs who had their teeth brushed at least three times a week had a 70% lower risk of periodontal disease (Vries et al., 2021).*

Next Up: How to Know Your Doodle's Routine is Working

Now that you have a clear grooming routine, how do you know the whole schedule is working?

In the next chapter, we'll look at:

- Key signs that your daily schedule is setting your Doodle up for success.

- What to tweak if things feel off—even with structure in place.

Turn the page to learn how to fine-tune your Doodle's routine for a happier, healthier life.

Chapter 19

Signs Your Schedule is Working and What to Adjust

How to Tell if Your Doodle's Routine is Balanced

S o you've implemented **The Doodle Daily Schedule Blueprint™—how can you tell it's working?**

Some signs are obvious—your Doodle is calmer, less reactive, and transitions smoothly between activities. But *success doesn't always look dramatic.* Sometimes, the *absence of frustration and chaos is the real sign that your routine is working.*

Realistic Signs That Your Routine Is Working

If you started this book feeling *overwhelmed,* the shift might be *subtle at first.* You may still have *moments of frustration,* but the big difference is:

- **Your Doodle is more predictable -** You're noticing patterns in when they settle, when they get excited, and when they need engagement.

- **They transition into rest more easily -** While they may still seek attention, they are beginning to self-settle more often instead of constantly pacing or barking.

- **Out-of-control Zoomies and demand barking still happen—but less often -** And when they do, they don't spiral into uncontrollable energy.

- **Vet and grooming visits are slightly easier** - They may not love it yet, but handling and exams are becoming more manageable.

- **Small schedule shifts don't throw them off as much** - A minor routine change doesn't result in total chaos—they may still react, but they recover faster.

These signs don't mean your Doodle is *perfectly behaved all the time*—but they *signal real progress toward a structured, balanced life.*

Case Study: From Overwhelmed to Enjoying Her Doodle Again

For months, Julia felt like **her entire day revolved around managing her Australian Labradoodle, Ollie.**

- She had spent so much energy stopping bad behaviors—barking at the window, counter-surfing, zooming through the house at night—that she never stopped to notice when those things weren't happening anymore.

- One night, she was sitting on the couch reading when she realized something: Ollie wasn't barking at her for attention or pacing the house looking for something to do. He was simply lying near her, chewing a toy.

- It hit her—things had changed. She wasn't exhausted from redirecting him every five minutes.

"I didn't notice at first because there wasn't a 'big moment.' It wasn't like he magically became perfect overnight. But when I looked back at how things used to be, I realized—he had settled into the routine. And I actually liked him again."

Key Takeaway:
Improvement isn't always about what your Doodle *does*—sometimes, it's about *what they're no longer doing.*

How to Fine-Tune Based on Energy, Behavior, or Life Stage

A structured routine provides *a foundation for success*, but your Doodle's *energy needs, attention span, and stress tolerance* change over time.

Need to Adjust Your Doodle's Routine?

If your Doodle's behavior has *shifted recently*, it might be time to *revisit key sections of this book* based on their current stage or challenges.

- **Started with a puppy?**

    ○ If your Doodle has entered adolescence, return to **Chapter 12: The Adolescent Doodle Schedule™ – Surviving the Teenage Phase** for impulse control strategies.

- **Your Doodle is maturing?**

    ○ If their energy levels are changing, check **Chapter 15: Customizing Your Doodle's Schedule for Your Lifestyle** to adjust routines for adulthood or senior years.

- **Added another dog?**

    ○ A second dog means a new household dynamic. Revisit **Chapter 14: Work-from-Home Life with a Doodle – Creating Structure** to manage multiple dogs without disrupting your schedule.

- **Experiencing unexpected setbacks?**

    ○ If potty training, crate training, or self-settling behaviors seem to be falling apart, revisit:

        - **Chapter 13: Potty Training Setbacks & Regression**

        - **Chapter 9: Crate Training & Schedules**

The Small Tweaks That Make a Big Difference

Studies show that *predictable routines enhance learning, lower stress levels, and improve problem-solving ability* (Horowitz, 2016; Hiby et al., 2006).

Even *small, strategic schedule tweaks* can create major improvements in focus and behavior.

1. Adjusting Exercise to Support Emotional Regulation

Many Doodle parents believe *more exercise = better behavior*, but research shows it's *the right kind of exercise and timing that matters.*

- High-arousal play too late in the day can increase evening restlessness instead of reducing it.

- Too much physical exercise without mental enrichment leads to higher endurance, not calmer behavior (*Blackwell et al., 2013*).

Tweak: Shift high-energy play to *earlier in the day* and replace evening play with *calm engagement activities* like puzzle feeders or decompression walks.

2. Using Mental Enrichment to Reduce Hyperactivity

Dogs experience decision fatigue, just like humans (*McGreevy et al., 2018*).

- If your Doodle struggles to settle, they may be mentally under-stimulated and seeking engagement through demand barking or pacing.

- A structured enrichment routine improves problem-solving and lowers frustration-based behaviors (*Horváth et al., 2020*).

Tweak: Increase **enrichment activities** such as:

- Scent work (sniffari walks, nosework games)

- Puzzle feeders and food-based problem-solving tasks

- Short, positive reinforcement training sessions (5-10 minutes each)

Final Thoughts: The Power of Small Changes

A well-structured daily routine is one of the most *powerful tools* for shaping your Doodle's behavior over time.

If something isn't working, the solution isn't necessarily more training—it's often a small adjustment in structure.

Your Doodle's behavior is a reflection of their environment and routine—and with structured adjustments, balance is always within reach.

What works today may need adjusting next month. What feels like a setback is often just part of the process. The best part? You now have the tools to tweak, adjust, and rebuild—whenever life changes.

Turn the page to explore bonus tools, training resources, and next steps in your Doodle journey.

Conclusion and Next Steps

How to Keep Building the Best Life for Your Doodle

You've made it to the end of this book—but in many ways, you're just getting started.

Raising a Doodle isn't about following a *rigid set of rules*. It's about understanding your dog's needs, finding what works best for your family, and adapting as life changes.

I designed **The Doodle Daily Schedule Blueprint™** to give you a *solid foundation*—a structure you can return to, adjust, and fine-tune as your Doodle grows.

Some days will feel effortless. Others? Not so much. And that's okay.

You're never failing—*just learning*. Together.

And the fact that you've taken the time to read this book, to truly understand your Doodle, and to create a routine that works for both of you? That already makes you the kind of Doodle parent every dog dreams of.

What Comes Next?

Your Doodle's needs *will evolve over time*, and their routine should evolve with them.

- **Puppyhood to Adolescence** - You'll need to adjust for impulse control and changing energy levels.

- **Adolescence to Adulthood -** It might be time to refine training expectations and balance mental and physical exercise differently.

- **Adulthood to Senior Years -** Lower-impact activities and joint-friendly adjustments will become more important.

Wherever you are in your Doodle journey, **you've built a strong foundation—and you now have the tools to adjust with confidence.**

If things ever feel off, just come back to *what you know works*: structured engagement, predictable transitions, and a routine that meets **both your needs and your Doodle's.**

Need a little help putting it all into action?

Your Doodle's Daily Schedule Companion Workbook is coming soon! It includes plug-and-play schedule templates, worksheets and logs, and the full Emergency Backup Toolkit to support you through travel, illness, or schedule chaos.

Perfect for real-life Doodle days—messy mornings and all. Join the waitlist to get it first at thedoodlepro.com/workbookwaitlist.

Ready to Dig Deeper? Join Me Inside The Doodle Pro® Academy!

If you want **ongoing guidance, live support, and step-by-step training tailored for Doodles**, The **Doodle Pro® Academy** is here for you.

Inside, you'll find:

- **Zoomies to Zen™ Comprehensive Doodle Course** A *six-week program* with over six hours of *Doodle-specific training videos* and exercises. You'll get *on-demand access plus live support* to customize your training for your unique Doodle.

- **Relaxation Protocol for Distractable Doodles™** A self-paced course featuring 15 *easy exercises* designed to *teach your Doodle how to relax, even in distracting environments*. The course is delivered in *a private podcast format*, so you can train anytime, anywhere.

Explore courses at: thedoodlepro.com/academy

Stay the Community & Stay Connected

For *ongoing learning, exclusive content, and live Q&As with expert trainers, groomers, vets, and more,* join **The Doodle Pro® Honor Society**.

Learn more at: thedoodlepro.com/membership

What Comes Next...

Doodle parenting is a lifelong journey, and I'm always working on new ways to support you.

If you've enjoyed this book, stay tuned for my next one—where I'll dive deeper into training and behavior solutions designed just for Doodles.

More details will be coming soon, and I can't wait to share it with you!

Let's Celebrate Your Doodle's Success!

One of my favorite things about my work is *seeing the happy, thriving Doodles of my readers and students.*

If this book has helped you, I'd *love* to see you and your Doodle in action!

Share a photo of your Doodle with the book and tag @TheDoodlePro on **Instagram or Facebook** @TheDoodlePro—your pup might even get featured!

Leave a Review, Help a Doodle Parent
If this Blueprint helped bring more peace, confidence, or clarity to your daily routine, would you take a minute to leave a review on Amazon or Goodreads?
Your words help other Doodle parents discover the support they need—and even a short review makes a big impact.
I read every single one, and your feedback means the world.
Thank you for being part of this mission to make life better for Doodles and the people who love them.

Join the conversation on The Doodle Pro® Podcast for expert interviews, training tips, and real-life Doodle advice on **Apple Podcasts, Spotify,** or wherever you love to listen.

Doodles are different—**wonderfully so.**™

And Doodle parents? **You're just as special.**

Thank you for **showing up with patience, love, and curiosity.**

Thank you for being part of **The Doodle Pro® community**.

Here's to years of **love, tail wags, and joyful moments** with your incredible Doodle.

If this Blueprint has made a positive difference for you and your Doodle, I would be grateful if you would take a moment to leave a review on Amazon. Just a single line helps other Doodle families discover this resource.

thedoodlepro.com/amazonreview

*Leave a review
on Amazon*

Your Next Step: The Doodle Pro® Roadmap

Looking for **more training, resources, or hands-on support?**

The next page includes a **Visual Roadmap** of all the courses, tools, and support available through **The Doodle Pro®**.

Turn the page to explore courses, tools, and next steps made just for you and your Doodle.

WAYS TO WORK WITH
THE DOODLE PRO®

Books

- **Your Doodle's Daily Schedule Blueprint-** *(Available now – create calm, connection, and structure for your pup)*
- **The Companion Workbook-** *(Coming soon– includes plug-and-play routines, worksheets and logs, & emergency plans)*
- **Raising the Perfect Doodle: Training & Behavior Solutions-** *(Full-length training guide in development– stay tuned!)*

Free Resources

- **Podcast-** Listen to The Doodle Pro® Podcast
- **Email List-** Exclusive training tips & updates
- **Social Media-** Follow for daily Doodle wisdom
- **Free Doodle Guides-** Download guides on Brushing, Treats, Relaxation, & *much* more!

COMMUNITY & MEMBERSHIP
(Ongoing Support & Coaching)

- **The Doodle Pro® Academy Honor Society Membership-** (Access to expert Vets, Trainers, & Groomers, live Q&As, exclusive community)
- **Doodle Parent Bootcamps-** (live training events)
- **Facebook Group-** (Engage, share, and learn from other Doodle parents!)

THE DOODLE PRO® ACADEMY
(Training & Courses)

- **Relaxation Protocol for Distractable Doodles™-** *(Private podcast-based training)*
- **Zoomies to Zen™-** *(Signature 6-week full training program, live support)*
- **Live Workshops & Webinars** *(One-time deep-dive sessions on common issues)*

Shop

- **Exclusive Doodle Parent Merch –** *Unique designs by Corinne for fellow Doodle lovers—nowhere else!*
- **Made for Doodle Devotees –** *Stylish, high-quality gear that celebrates your one-of-a-kind pup!*

Quick Reference Guide

Your At-a-Glance Guide to Daily Schedules, Training, and Troubleshooting

B uilding a great routine for your Doodle isn't about *rigid rules*—it's about *structure, predictability, and flexibility* as their needs evolve.

> Use this **Quick Reference Guide** *to find key training topics, daily schedules, and troubleshooting advice—fast.*

Get printable versions of all of the schedules, trackers, and charts mentioned in this book—family-friendly and fridge-ready.

Download your copy at:

thedoodlepro.com/bonustoolkit

Pro Tip: Print out your puppy's schedule, training reminders, or troubleshooting flowcharts and post them in a visible spot (like the fridge!) so the whole family can stay consistent.

Daily Schedules and Routine Adjustment

The Doodle Daily Schedule Blueprint™ ◻ *Chapter 3*

- How to create a structured, flexible daily schedule that balances engagement, rest, and training.

Morning Routine – Preventing Chaos and Zoomies ◻ *Chapter 4*

- Step-by-step **Doodle Morning Flow™** to start the day calmly and avoid overstimulation.

Midday Reset – Avoiding Barking & Restlessness ◻ *Chapter 5*

- **Doodle Midday Reset™** to prevent demand barking, destructive behaviors, and midday meltdowns.

Evening Wind-Down – Preventing Nighttime Zoomies ◻ *Chapter 6*

- Structured **Doodle Evening Wind-Down™** routine to promote relaxation before bed.

Customizing Your Doodle's Schedule for Life Changes ◻ *Chapter 15*

- Adjusting routines for seasonal shifts, travel, school schedules, or unexpected disruptions.

Puppy Training and Development

New Puppy Starter Schedule (8 Weeks - 6 Months) ◻ *Chapter 7*

- Puppy-specific daily schedule to prevent overstimulation, zoomies, and frustration-based behaviors.

Potty Training and Preventing Accidents ◻ *Chapter 8*

- A structured potty training schedule with troubleshooting tips for setbacks.

Crate Training and Alone Time Confidence ◻ *Chapter 9*

- Teaching your puppy to love their crate and prevent separation stress.

Socialization and Preventing Sensory Overload ◻ *Chapter 10*

- The **Doodle Socialization Blueprint™**—how to introduce new experiences the right way without overstimulation.

Behavior and Impulse Control

Managing Overstimulation & Stress Signals ◻ *Chapter 11*

- How to identify and manage stress behaviors before they escalate.

Surviving the Adolescent Doodle Phase (6-18 Months) ◻ *Chapter 12*

- The **Adolescent Doodle Schedule™**—why they "forget" their training and how to reinforce impulse control.

Potty Training Regression and Accidents ◻ *Chapter 13*

- Why previously house-trained Doodles may regress—and how to quickly reset their training.

Preventing Demand Barking and Work-From-Home Strategies ◻ *Chapter 14*

- How to teach your Doodle to settle while you work and stop attention-seeking barking.

Vet, Grooming and Long-Term Care

Vet and Vaccination Schedule – Preventative Care ◻ *Chapter 17*

- Age-based vaccination and wellness schedule to stay on top of routine care.

Grooming Schedule – Preventing Matting & Maintaining Coat Health □ *Chapter 18*

- How often to brush, bathe, and groom your Doodle to prevent coat and skin issues.

Signs Your Routine Is Working & What to Adjust

Recognizing When Your Doodle's Routine Is Working □ *Chapter 19*

- Subtle signs that your schedule is working—even if you don't notice right away.

- How to fine-tune your routine as your Doodle grows and their needs change.

Final Encouragement and Next Steps □ *Conclusion*

- How to stay flexible and continue reinforcing good habits.

- Where to go for ongoing learning, support, and troubleshooting.

Further Listening

For expert insights from *top trainers, groomers, veterinarians, and behaviorists,* listen to **The Doodle Pro® Podcast**, where science-backed guidance is tailored for Doodle parents. **Listen now on Apple Podcasts, Spotify,** or wherever you enjoy your podcasts.

Podcast Episodes Referenced

Training and Behavior

- **#32 & #33 Separation Anxiety & How to Fix It-** *Interview with Malena DeMartini-Price*

- #75 **Crate Training Done Right**- *Interview with Malena DeMartini-Price*

- **#60 Enrichment & Preventing Problem Behaviors**- *Interview with Zazie Todd*

Puppy Socialization & Adult Doodle Confidence

- **#53 & #54 Puppy Socialization Done Right**-*Interview with Marge Rogers & Eileen Anderson*

- **#64 Adult Doodle Socialization & Confidence Building**- *Interview with Marge Rogers & Eileen Anderson*

- **#15 Doodle Brain Under Construction: Understanding & Training Through Adolescence**

Grooming & Care

- **#3 The Groomer's Perspective on Doodle Coat Care**- *Interview with grooming expert River Lee*

- **#47 & #49 Stress-Free Doodle Care**- *Interview with Laura Monaco Torelli*

Don't miss a single episode! Subscribe today on **Apple Podcasts, Spotify,** or your favorite podcast platform.

Need More Help?

Want expert support, step-by-step programs, or coaching with me, The Doodle Pro®?

Explore **The Doodle Pro® Academy™** courses. *Start today at:* **thedoodlepro.com/academy**

Need real-time support? Join **The Doodle Pro® Honor Society™** for live Q&As with trainers, vets, and groomers, and me, **The Doodle Pro®.** *Learn more at:* **thedoodlepro.com/membership**

For printable schedules, training charts, and behavior trackers, visit: thedoodlepro.com/bonustoolkit

References & Additional Reading

U nderstanding your Doodle's unique needs is a journey, and ongoing learning can deepen your bond while improving their training and care. The following books, scientific studies, and expert resources provide science-backed guidance on canine behavior, training, and emotional well-being.

Understanding Canine Behavior

Clothier, Suzanne. 2002. *Bones Would Rain from the Sky: Deepening Our Relationships with Dogs.* New York: Warner Books.

Todd, Zazie. 2020. *Wag: The Science of Making Your Dog Happy.* Vancouver: Greystone Books.

Waggoner, Lisa Lyle. *Understanding Dog Body Language.* Cold Nose College.

Puppy Socialization & Early Development

American Veterinary Society of Animal Behavior (AVSAB). 2008. Position Statement on Puppy Socialization.

Rogers, Marge, and Eileen Anderson. 2021. *Puppy Socialization: What It Is and How to Do It.* First Stone Publishing.

Separation Anxiety & Crate Training

DeMartini-Price, Malena. 2014. *Treating Separation Anxiety in Dogs.* Wenatchee, WA: Dogwise Publishing.

Tuber, D. S., S. Sanders, M. B. Hennessy, & A. Miller. 2005. "Behavioral and Physiological Responses of Dogs to Separation from Their Caregivers." *Physiology & Behavior* 84 (2): 233-239.

Canine Cognition & Emotional Sensitivity

Kaminski, Juliane, Lisa Schulz, and Michael Tomasello. 2012. "How Dogs Know What We Know: A Study of Dog Cognition and Perspective-Taking." *Animal Cognition* 15 (2): 295–304.

McGreevy, P. D., M. J. Starling, N. J. Branson, M. L. Cobb, and D. Calnon. 2018. "An Overview of Canine Neurobiology and Cognition: Implications for Training and Behavior." *Applied Animal Behaviour Science* 204: 1-18.

The Role of Predictable Routines in Reducing Stress

Hiby, E. F., N. J. Rooney, and J. W. S. Bradshaw. 2006. "Dog Training Methods: Their Use, Effectiveness, and Interaction with Behavior and Welfare." *Animal Welfare* 15 (1): 63–69.

Hiby, E. F., N. J. Rooney, and J. W. S. Bradshaw. 2022. "The Impact of Routine Changes on Canine Behavior and Emotional Health." *Journal of Veterinary Behavior* 52 (4): 17-25. Koolhaas, J. M., A. Bartolomucci, B. Buwalda, S. F. de Boer, G. Flügge, S. M. Korte, P. Meerlo, R. Murison, B. Olivier, P. Palanza, G. Richter-Levin, A. Sgoifo, T. Steimer, O. Stiedl, G. van Dijk, M. Wöhr, and E. Fuchs. 2011. "Stress Revisited: A Critical Evaluation of the Stress Concept." *Neuroscience & Biobehavioral Reviews* 35 (5): 1291-1301.

Duhigg, C. 2012. *The Power of Habit: Why We Do What We Do in Life and Business.* New York: Random House.

Decision Fatigue & Mental Stimulation in Dogs

DVM360. 2021. "Jumpstart Your Brain: Fight Against Decision Fatigue." *DVM360 Magazine.*

Overtired Puppies & Hyperactivity

Kovács, K., A. Kis, M. Gácsi, and J. Topál. 2023. "ADHD-Like Behavior in Family Dogs Is Associated with Sleep Quality." *Scientific Reports* 13 (1): 28263.

The Science of Exercise & Mental Stimulation

Blackwell, E. J., R. A. Casey, and J. W. S. Bradshaw. 2013. "The Relationship Between Training Methods and Problem Behaviors in Dogs." *Journal of Veterinary Behavior* 8 (6): 370–376.

Horowitz, Alexandra. 2016. *Being a Dog: Following the Dog into a World of Smell.* New York: Scribner.

The Myth of the "Alpha Dog" & Positive Training

American Veterinary Society of Animal Behavior (AVSAB). 2021. *Position Statement on Humane Dog Training.*

Donaldson, Jean. 1996. *The Culture Clash: A Revolutionary New Way of Understanding the Relationship Between Humans and Domestic Dogs.* James & Kenneth Publishers.

Mech, L. David. 1999. "Alpha Status, Dominance, and Division of Labor in Wolf Packs." *Canadian Journal of Zoology* 77 (8): 1196–1203.

Expert Training & Grooming Resources

Stephens, Laura. The Nerdy Nail Trimmer (YouTube Channel)

Monaco Torelli, Laura. *Animal Behavior Training Concepts.*

The Doodle Pro® Podcast
For expert interviews on **training, grooming, behavior, and care**, listen to **The Doodle Pro® Podcast**, featuring leading trainers, veterinarians, and industry professionals.
Listen now on Apple Podcasts, Spotify, or wherever you enjoy your podcasts.

Stay Supported on Your Doodle Journey

Before we wrap up, don't forget to grab your **Daily Doodle Toolkit™**—your free, reader-only bonus designed to keep your routine strong long after the last page.

Your Toolkit Includes:

• **Full-color printable schedules** – Morning, Midday & Evening routines

• **Potty, grooming & vet care checklists** – Fridge-friendly and family-proof

• **Reader-only discounts** – Trusted tools and enrichment picks I personally use

Visit **thedoodlepro.com/bonustoolkit** or scan the QR code below to download instantly.

*Scan this with your smartphone's camera
to download your bonus digital Toolkit!*

You've got the plan—now grab the tools to follow through with confidence.

With appreciation, Corinne Gearhart *The Doodle Pro®*

About the Author

Corinne and her Cavapoo Nestlé in the Colorado mountains.

"Doodles are different, wonderfully so. That's exactly why I've dedicated my career to understanding them inside and out."

Corinne Gearhart, known as The Doodle Pro®, is a **certified dog trainer and educator** who has spent over 50,000 hours working exclusively with Doodles, helping their families raise happier, better-behaved companions. Through her industry first Doodle-exclusive boarding and training program, she studied training methods in real-time, refining proven, science-backed strategies tailored to Doodles' unique needs.

She's the founder of The Doodle Pro® Podcast—an internationally **top-ranked podcast**—and the popular The Doodle Pro® Academy, where she has helped thousands of Doodle parents worldwide build stronger bonds, establish better routines, and prevent common behavior struggles. Her down-to-earth expertise has made her a trusted voice in the Doodle community, guiding overwhelmed puppy parents and experienced dog owners alike.

Passionate about positive reinforcement and force-free training, Corinne specializes in addressing the quirks that make Doodles both delightful and challenging—whether it's their poodle-like intelligence, retriever-like enthusiasm, or their deep emotional sensitivity. She believes that understanding a Doodle's unique needs is the key to unlocking a well-mannered, confident companion.

When she's not coaching Doodle parents or developing new training resources, Corinne enjoys traveling—**and usually ends up photographing dogs more than landmarks.** A lifelong creative, even her artwork finds its way back to Doodles. She shares her home with her two sons and Nestlé, her beloved Cavapoo, who reminds her daily that Doodles truly are different—wonderfully so.

For behind the scenes looks at her work with Doodles or to connect with Corinne, follow her on Instagram and Facebook **@TheDoodlePro**.